DAVID ATTENBOROUGH

A LiFE STORY

Lizzie Huxley-Jones

Illustrated by Sarah Papworth

SCHOLASTIC

For Dylan & Theo.

First published in the UK by Scholastic Children's Books, 2020
Euston House, 24 Eversholt Street, London, NW1 1DB

A division of Scholastic Limited
London ~ New York ~ Toronto ~ Sydney ~ Auckland
Mexico City ~ New Delhi ~ Hong Kong

SCHOLASTIC and associated logos are trademarks and/or registered
trademarks of Scholastic Inc.

Text © Lizzie Huxley-Jones, 2020
Illustrations by Sarah Papworth

The right of Lizzie Huxley-Jones to be identified as the author of this
work has been asserted by them in accordance with the
Copyright, Designs and Patents Act, 1988.

ISBN 978 0702 30287 9

Any website addresses listed in the book are correct at the time of going to
print. However, please be aware that online content is subject to change and
websites can contain or offer content that is unsuitable for children.
We advise all children be supervised when using the Internet.

Printed and bound by CPI Group (UK) Ltd, Croydon, CR0 4YY

Papers used by Scholastic Children's Books are made from wood grown in
sustainable forests.

1 3 5 7 9 10 8 6 4 2

www.scholastic.co.uk

CONTENTS

INTRODUCTION

Have you ever turned on the television to watch a natural history programme?

You might have seen wildebeest ranging across the savannah, or schools of silvery fish escaping birds and dolphins, or even weird and wonderful plants flowering. But it's not just the images themselves; the stories captivate us and introduce us to the secrets of the natural world.

Thanks to the power of technology, most of us are able to access the natural world from wherever we are; through photos, images and television programmes. And many of these programmes are narrated by a very recognizable hushed and gentle voice – that of Sir David Attenborough.

But David Attenborough isn't just a famous voiceover artist. He is a pioneer of natural history filmmaking who not only established the way nature appears on television but also shaped early television itself as a producer. He has produced and presented over twenty blockbuster documentary series focusing on the various aspects of life on our planet, taking us on the adventures with him. In the very early days, they even included the occasional shot of him hiding behind plants waiting for the animals to arrive! You could even say he is a storyteller, revealing the secrets of the natural world to viewers at home with his trademark style.

Now in his nineties, he is well-known for all things nature, and considered one of the most loved public figures in the UK. He has over thirty honorary degrees from universities throughout the world – more than any other person – and has a part of the Natural History Museum in London dedicated to him. Over twenty species and genera (a grouping classification that sits between "family" and "species") have been named after him, including weevils, fossilised fish, flowering trees, parasites of deep-sea fish and even echidnas – also referred to as "spiny anteaters".

In recent years, his focus has shifted from making programmes about wildlife and the beauty of nature to showcasing the impacts we are having on our world with more environmental messaging. *Blue Planet II*'s (2017) episodes on ocean pollution led people all over the world to move towards using less single-use plastic, and his 2019 series, *Our Planet*, which launched on Netflix, was viewed by 33 million people worldwide.

But how did a bug-hunting, fossil-finding boy from Leicester grow to become one of the most recognizable humans on nature television? In this book, we're not only going to look at how David Attenborough brought the world into our living rooms, we're going to explore the world along with him.

IN THE BEGINNING...

David Frederick Attenborough was born on 8 May 1926 in West London, to parents, Frederick and Mary.

The world of the 1920s was very different from how things are today. The First World War had ended in 1918, after which there was a period of mass unemployment and even national strikes by the later years of the 1920s.

Plus, you only had to go to school until you were fourteen.

Growing up, he was the middle child of three brothers, with Richard the eldest and John the youngest. While John ended up working in the car industry, both Richard and David found themselves in film and television. If you are a fan of old films, you may even have seen Richard in them – to me, he will always be John Hammond, the owner of Jurassic Park in the 1993 film.

Young David with brothers

Animals were always a big part of David's life. As a child he kept a tank full of tropical fish and one of his favourite activities as a teenager was cycling around in search of fossils in the wild, coming back with pockets full of rocks. He had a whole collection of feathers, bird eggs and shells that he would show off.

Their father, Frederick, was the principal of University College, Leicester, and so David and his brothers spent much of their childhoods roaming the halls. David even found himself a little side job there. The local biology department were in desperate need of newts for their research, and so David offered himself up to provide them with a regular supply as they required. What they didn't know was that the newts David sold them were coming from a pond on their own grounds!

David carried his love of animals to Cambridge University, where he studied Natural Sciences, focusing on geology and zoology. Geology is the study of the earth itself, and the materials and structures from which it is made – rocks, minerals, metals, oil and fossils. Meanwhile, zoology is the study of animals. Back then, it was very much about animals in laboratory experiments and looking at their bodies. David dreamed of watching animals in the wild and learning about them in their own environments, but science was a long way off from studying animals that way. He knew he wanted to do something with animals in the future but didn't know exactly what.

While at university, he fell in love with a Welsh woman named Jane Elizabeth Ebsworth Oriel, and she would later become his wife.

He finished his studies in 1947, only two years after the Second World War had ended, and mandatory National Service had been introduced in the UK, which meant that all young able-bodied men aged between eighteen and twenty-five had to serve eighteen months in the armed forces. David joined the army and, much to his disappointment, was posted in Scotland. He had been hoping for adventures further afield.

When his National Service was over, he worked for an educational publisher making books for children but didn't feel like it was quite the right job for him. He saw a job advert in the newspaper seeking someone to produce radio programmes for the British Broadcasting Corporation, or, as you might know it, the BBC. He applied and waited, hoping that he'd be able to move on to something new soon. A few weeks later, David got a polite rejection note in the post. There was nothing he could do, so he continued on at the educational publisher until, eventually, he got a phone call offering him a golden opportunity: the chance to work in television. A woman named Mary Adams who worked in the television department had seen his application, and felt that he might be a good fit for their department instead.

And so, in September 1952, David found himself quitting his job in educational publishing and attending a training course that taught him about all aspects of broadcast television. A few months later he began his career in making television programmes, as an assistant producer.

THE BBC

The British Broadcasting Corporation, or BBC, is an international public services broadcaster based in London, producing television and radio content and transmitting it throughout the world.

The BBC started out in the 1920s making radio programmes, and eventually moved into television. They are the world's oldest national broadcasting organisation and one of the biggest.

THE TIMELINE OF TV

When David started his career at the BBC in the 1950s, television was very different from how it is today. There were no streaming services to pick and choose from and there were very few computers, and the ones that were available looked nothing like those you see now. There wasn't even any Internet! There was only one channel and it was in black and white.

Television came about when, in 1924, a young Scottish engineer named John Logie Baird, based in Hastings, built a machine in his attic that could transmit a still image a few yards. The first television or "televisor" was made up of a rotating disc surrounded by holes that you would shine a beam of light

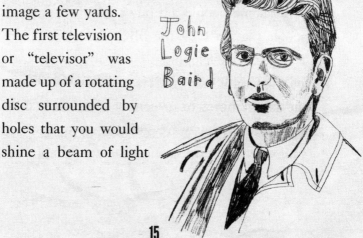

John Logie Baird

through in order to project an image.

The televisions looked very different from the flat-screen TVs most of us have in our homes today. They usually looked like a wardrobe or a large wooden box with a very small screen, and projected an image the size of a stamp that the glass would magnify to twice the size. You would have to sit very close to it to see what was going on! They were also huge and expensive, which meant only rich people or eager engineers had them in their homes.

Many people were extremely excited by this invention and Baird was invited to exhibit it in London. It was still a long way away from being the televisions we know today, and people largely saw it as an interesting experiment rather than something they could one day have in their home.

But some people did buy a televisor. Enough people that, in 1929, the BBC allowed the Baird Television Development Company to use their medium-wave transmitters to broadcast images and programmes to owners of these early TVs, instead of the low-wave signals they were using. These early transmissions were often simple, but by 1930 they were able to match up the sounds and pictures in their broadcasts. It was, of course, still all in black and white, and very poor quality. Actors had to wear very strange bright makeup in yellows, blues and greens so that it would show up on screen, and for two actors to fit on screen they had to sit with barely an inch between them!

By 1936, things had come a long way. Televisions themselves were smaller and had slightly larger screens. The BBC was the first publicly available television service in the world, using the most advanced technology of the time, which was still grainy black-and-white pictures made of 405 horizontal lines, transmitted on the high-frequency waveband.

The BBC moved to a new headquarters at Alexandra Palace in London where they had two small studios inside a very grand-looking building that sat atop a big hill surrounded by a concert hall, theatres and a huge park. Here they launched their own first "high-definition" broadcast (though this was nothing compared to high definition today!), but even then, this only aired for an hour from 3 p.m. and from 7 or 9 p.m.

every day! Not only that, but you could only pick up the transmissions on your TV if you lived in Birmingham or London, meaning it wasn't accessible to everyone.

BBC Alexandra Palace

The cameras used to film were big metal contraptions on bicycle wheels, and there were no digital screens for the camera operator to use, just a single viewfinder that showed the image in colour and upside down. They only had one lens and were known to break down regularly.

There were three in each studio and on occasion all three would stop working, and viewers at home would be shown a reel of stock footage, like waves on the shore or kittens playing with wool.

One of the first big challenges for early TV was the coronation of Queen Elizabeth II's parents, King George VI and Queen Elizabeth, in 1937. The procession was filmed on only three cameras using a single outdoor studio inside a van, but was almost not aired at all because – just as the procession came around the corner at Marble Arch – all the equipment went dead! Luckily they were able to get things working in time by giving the equipment an "almighty biff".

All television programmes were live, and there was no teleprompter to help presenters remember their lines. Sometimes people would be caught on camera checking their scripts or being given a prompt, but viewers didn't mind too much when it was all so new, and they enjoyed that it was airing live from the studios. The technology to record programmes didn't exist for a long time, and when it became available, it was very expensive to do, so very few programmes from this time period exist in the BBC Archives.

However, the big TV experiment quickly ground to a halt with the outbreak of the Second World War in 1939, and television transmissions were suspended until the war ended in 1945. They promised to come back when the war was over and when transmissions did return, viewers at home set up their TVs and found the first broadcast shown to be the same one that had been abruptly cut off before war began.

By the time David started working at the BBC in 1952, the technology hadn't changed much at all. They were using the same cameras, the same two studios, and were still only able to show live programmes, which as you'll find out, often caused havoc...

SECOND WORLD WAR

- The Second World War was fought between two groups of countries we now refer to as the Axis and Allied Powers. It started when Germany invaded Poland in September 1939.

- The Allies were Britain and many countries in the Commonwealth including Australia, New Zealand and India, as well as Poland, France, the Union of Soviet Socialist Republics (USSR), the USA, China, the Netherlands, Yugoslavia, Belgium and Greece.

- The Axis were Germany, Italy, Japan, Hungary, Bulgaria and Romania (and Finland was allied with them too).

- One of the main reasons a world war broke out had to do with the rise of Nazism in Germany and many Germans believed that, after the First World War, they were treated harshly to make up for the costs and damage of the war. For example, they were forced to pay a hefty fine and to give up land and territories.

- In Germany, the ruling party was the National Socialist German Workers' Party, or the Nazis, led by Adolf Hitler. The Nazis were a far-right fascist party who believed in dictatorship, which means a ruler who has total power over a country, and who usually gets this power through force. They believed white people were the "Master Race" and saw non-whites as inferior. They were also anti-Semitic, which is prejudice targeted at Jewish people, blaming them for Germany losing the First World War.

- These beliefs led to the Holocaust; the systematic imprisonment and murder of millions of Jews, disabled people, political opponents, LGBTQ people, and Romany communities.

- Over 70 million people died in the war, which is more people than live in the United Kingdom in 2020.

- The United Nations, a collaboration between countries, was formed after the war to foster peace and prevent large wars breaking out ever again – there are now 193 member countries.

THE QUEST BEGINS

David's love of animals was still very much on his mind at the BBC, and he was keen to work on programmes that featured them. He worked on a number of slightly strange programmes, such as an interview with a famous scientist who was pooped on by a goose, a ballet about a fishmonger in love, and a panel programme called *Animal, Vegetable, Mineral?* where experts had to guess what a strange object they were given could be. But what else could he make? He had been on camera a handful of times as a stand-in but was told (by Mary Adams, the woman who hired him!) he didn't quite have a face for television as his teeth were "too big". He decided it was best to stay behind the scenes.

One of the most popular programmes at the time was presented by George Cansdale, one of the top zookeepers at London Zoo. He would bring along small animals to the studio and would talk all about them to the viewers at home. The programme was aired live, so mishaps often occurred – one time a small African squirrel decided it had had quite enough of being on TV and escaped into the air vents! The staff tried to capture it, but it managed to slip away for several days. Occasionally, it would even pop its head out to make a guest appearance on the other programmes that were filming!

David decided to try out a more scientific series of programmes, presented by famous scientist Julian Huxley, which was more educational but perhaps not quite as fun as the spectacle of seeing animals up to mischief in the studio.

Viewers loved these TV programmes, and it gave young David an idea – what about a programme that combined footage of animals in their own habitats with live explanations from the studio?

"IF THERE WERE A FEW UNAVOIDABLE INCIDENTS, SUCH AS AN ESCAPE OR A BITE, THEN SO MUCH THE BETTER."

David realized he needed someone from London Zoo to help him develop the programme. He contacted his friend, Jack Lester, who was the curator of the Reptile House at London Zoo. David imagined each episode showing footage of Jack searching for animals in the wild and then cutting back to the studio where Jack would present the animals they caught and talk about them.

The animals would then go to live in London Zoo. This style of going to other countries to explore and collect animals to fill up zoos is a very old one that gained popularity in the Victorian era – we know now that this is not the right way to do it, and there are many people who believe animals should not be held in captivity at all.

They decided to pitch their idea to the BBC and London Zoo together over lunch at the zoo's restaurant. It was going to be a very expensive TV programme – the cost of filming on location alone was going to be high, but they'd also have to cover travel, accommodation, the equipment and then the shipping of all the animals back to the zoo. Worried that they would be told no, Jack and David cunningly told Mary Adams from the BBC that the London Zoo rep had already agreed to it, and told the London Zoo rep that the BBC had already agreed to it. This led to both organizations signing up to the exciting new project, all because they thought the other had already signed up!

Choosing their first destination was an easy choice for Jack and David. It had to be Sierra Leone, West Africa. Jack knew the country well and had lived there for a while, and so was confident he could get them around and find the animals they needed.

So, they found themselves in a position where they had the money and they had the destination country, but what about the animals? This was a quest, after all, but a quest for what? David and Jack were keen to find something people in the UK wouldn't have seen before and that London Zoo would want to keep. They decided they would go in search of the white-necked rockfowl, but worried that the bird alone didn't sound particularly exciting and so they decided to simply call the programme *Zoo Quest*.

LONDON ZOO AND ZOOS TODAY

London Zoo opened in 1828 and is one of the oldest zoos in the world. Run by the Zoological Society of London, London Zoo aimed to collect and keep animals for scientific study, but also so that the public could come to see the animals and learn about them too.

The first creatures they had included an orangutan, Arabian oryx and greater kudus, and the quagga and thylacine, both sadly now extinct. This means there are no more of these animals left alive in the wild or in captivity. London was also the first zoo in the world to have its own aquarium and reptile house.

The zoo is still open today, though it has changed a lot since it opened, as zookeepers have grown to learn more about the animals.

For instance, all the animals were kept indoors until 1902, because everyone thought they would get too cold. The zookeepers soon realized that the animals adapted quickly, and often liked the fresh air and more room to roam.

The initial enclosures were usually quite bare, with nothing to entertain the captive animal. At zoos today, you might have seen food hidden around their enclosures to encourage foraging, or toys or climbing structures for them to play with. This is referred to as "animal enrichment" and is considered a very important aspect of looking after all animals.

We also now know that animals do much better if their enclosure looks more like their home environment. For example, the building containing the enclosure for the nocturnal and sound-sensitive bush baby is very low lit, with signs asking visitors to be quiet and patient.

One of the biggest changes is that people no longer go out on expeditions to capture animals to be shipped back to live at the zoo. This is because removing rare animals from the wild puts more pressure on the rest of the species to survive. Another reason is that, over the years, most attitudes towards this have changed; people generally think it is unkind – and even wrong – to remove an animal from its home simply for our benefit and entertainment.

So, how *do* zoos get new animals now?

Every species in captivity has a record of how many animals are in zoos, and who their siblings and parents might be. This is called a "studbook" and means that when zoos decide to breed their animals or transfer them to different zoos, they can keep track of who is related to whom. As there are only so many of each species in zoos – this is important to prevent them breeding within their own families, as this can cause serious health problems for the animals.

Nowadays, it's only when a species is considered endangered and there are very few left in the wild that scientists consider taking them into captivity. When this happens, breeding programmes are a top priority, to try to breed enough animals to support the wild populations. We call this a captive breeding programme. One of the most well-known successes of captive breeding is the Arabian oryx – a type of antelope.

THE ARABIAN ORYX

The Arabian oryx lived on the Arabian Peninsula, but by the 1970s they had been hunted so much that there were very few of them left in the wild. We call this being "extinct in the wild", which means the breeding population is so low and threats against them so big that zoologists don't think the species will ever recover.

Luckily, the Phoenix Zoo in Arizona had begun a breeding programme for the Arabian

oryx in the 1960s starting with only nine oryx.
Over 200 babies were born and shared with
zoos around the world in order to breed with the
oryx they already had.

Whole herds of oryx were kept in these zoos,
until the 1980s, when the first oryx were
reintroduced to Oman. There are now over 1,000
Arabian oryx in the wild across Oman, Saudi
Arabia and Israel. However, their population is
still under threat from illegal hunting
(also called "poaching"),
and habitat destruction
caused by drilling for oil.

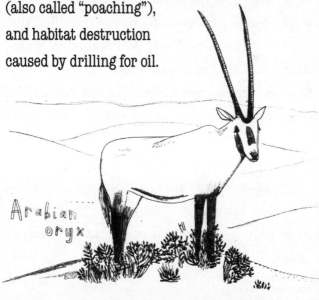

Arabian
oryx

THE QUEST
TO SIERRA LEONE

The first-ever *Zoo Quest* was a challenge for the team. It was 1954, and no one had ever made a programme like it before.

Filming in Sierra Leone was a huge technological challenge for the young team. In the London studios, the suitcase-sized cameras were normally mounted on huge tripods and used 35mm film (which means the film that went into the camera was 35 millimetres wide), which came in large rolls. These cameras filmed live, and the programme was put out through the control room attached to the studio. That would stay the same for the in-studio bits, but what about the in-country filming?

David knew they had to try something different – smaller cameras and narrower 16-millimetre-wide film. That made it much easier to record images of the animals in the wild to bring back.

These cameras couldn't record sound as well, so they would have to record that separately. The cameras also had to be wound up every forty seconds to make them work, but he knew this would be the best option they had for filming animals in the wild.

However, the camera operators at the BBC looked down their nose at this basic equipment, thinking the footage would be rubbish quality, and refused to help. Luckily a plucky filmmaker, Charles Lagus, was up to the task. He had just returned from a failed expedition to find the mythical Abominable Snowman and was keen to go off on a new adventure.

Charles
Lagus

THE ABOMINABLE SNOWMAN

The Abominable Snowman, or Yeti, is a very large mythical creature, thought to live in the Himalayas. Its appearance is often described as ape-like and many drawings show them as having white or brown fur.

Large human-like footprints have been sighted on and around Mount Everest during various expeditions since the 1800s. A few people have even claimed to see a tall creature walking on two feet!

Several groups returning from expeditions have produced "scalps" of yetis, but these generally have turned out to be fakes – usually the fur of a small deer-like or goat-like animal called the goral.

Though most people agree the Abominable Snowman is probably just some big footprints and a good story, you never know what strange creatures are yet to be discovered!

The next piece of the puzzle was someone to look after the animals. Even though Jack was an expert at catching the animals and knew a lot about how to feed and care for them in captivity, it was obvious they would need an extra pair of hands. The head keeper for London Zoo's birdhouse, Alf Woods, agreed to join the adventure and so the team set off for Sierra Leone in September 1954.

SIERRA LEONE

Where it is: West Africa

Capital: Freetown

Climate: tropical, hot and humid with a summer rainy season and a winter dry season

Population: 7.7 million people

Languages: English, Krio, Mende, Temne, Arabic and many other indigenous languages.

The first animals they came across were marching columns of driver ants. They would parade past, carrying parts of creatures that the ants at the front of the procession had caught and killed,

A trail of driver ants

accompanied by huge black soldier ants that protected the group. They were bringing food back to their queen and the rest of the worker ants; the nest was close to where David and the team stayed at a research station owned by an agricultural department. As they quietly watched the ants, David began to notice tiny dramas and stories taking place. He wondered, what if all their films could be a kind of story?

The film crew carried watercolour illustrations of all the animals they hoped to see, to show local people in the hope that they might be able to identify them. As well as the white-necked rockfowl, the zoo wanted other small birds, chimpanzees, black-and-white colobus monkeys, huge termite mounds and some species of fish.

The agricultural instructor at a village they visited recognized the bird in the drawings and told them where they might find them, high up in the forest. A few villagers were reluctant to accompany them as there was a local belief that these birds were the servants of a giant devil that lived inside the boulders they nested on. Luckily, David and the team found some willing guides who helped them locate two nests on the underside of a huge boulder. Inside one of them was a clutch of eggs. The group decided to come back two weeks later, in the hope that the eggs would have hatched.

Their gamble paid off. On their second visit, they were lucky enough to see a pair of white-necked rockfowl feeding their newly hatched chicks. They stayed for many days watching and filming the birds and then, with the efforts for London Zoo in mind, the team took one young chick back with them to camp.

Even though they knew quite a lot about the rockfowl and how to care for it, the little chick refused to eat for the first few days. They tried all sorts of insects, but no luck. Everyone was worried – this little bird was the whole reason they had come to Sierra Leone, and they were scared that if it didn't eat, it might die! Then, Jack had an idea. The birds lived along rivers and streams; perhaps it might like to eat a little frog? To their delight, the tiny bird ate it up greedily and chirped for seconds. The crew spent much of the next few days catching lots of frogs as they came to realize the little chick could eat up to a dozen a day! Luckily, Jack was able to encourage the chick on to a diet of mealworms, which made the journey home much easier and meant much less clambering around in ponds for the team.

THE WHITE-NECKED ROCKFOWL
Picathartes gymnocephalus
(pick-a-thart-ees gym-no-sef-a-less)
The white-necked rockfowl is a small bird with dark black-brown wings and tail, a white neck and body, and a featherless head that is black and bright sunshine yellow. It almost looks like it's wearing a superhero mask over its eyes to disguise itself.

The birds are found in several countries in West Africa, including Côte d'Ivoire, Ghana, Guinea, Liberia and, of course, Sierra Leone. They are usually found in rocky areas of forests and often live close to streams and rivers, as they use mud as a building material for their nests, along with leaves, twigs and whatever else they can find. They tend to build their nests on the undersides of large boulders so that they are protected from any rain.

The White-necked Rockfowl

They mainly eat insects such as grasshoppers, ants and even cockroaches, but are also known to vary their diet a little to include frogs, small lizards and centipedes. Delicious!

They have a strange call that sounds somewhere between a hen clucking and a pig oinking.

According to the IUCN Red List, there are fewer than 10,000 of these birds left in the wild, as burning forests to clear them for farmland removes their habitat.

The baby rockfowl wasn't the only young animal the *Zoo Quest* team would be bringing back. They had ground squirrels, African squirrels – one of which David would pop into his pocket to keep warm – tiny baby bush rats and even a young chimpanzee that would sit in Jack's lap and drink bottles of milk, whom they named Jane.

After two months in Sierra Leone, the team loaded their menagerie on to a truck and drove back to Freetown, where they had booked a space on a freight plane for them and all the animals.

They returned to London triumphant, and all the animals settled into their new homes at London Zoo. The first-ever programme was shown in December 1954, with Jack presenting the animals and David cueing up the footage and cameras from the control room. A large audience (for that time) started tuning in every week, and people on the street were beginning to recognize David from TV. Before the series had finished airing, a London bus driver even wound down his window to ask him if they were ever going to find the bird!

Sadly, Jack suddenly became unwell soon after the first episode, and that meant he couldn't do the live part of the programme for the second episode. David realized that it was up to him, as he was the only one who knew all the animals. He took Jack's place in the studio, not only for that episode, but for the rest of the series.

TO SOUTH AMERICA!

Eight weeks after the last *Zoo Quest* programme had aired on TV, David Attenborough and the team were eager to leave for their second expedition.

David was determined their next series would be on a new continent, and suggested they choose a country in South America. They picked Guyana, then called British Guiana, which was part of the Commonwealth.

GUYANA

Where it is: South America

Capital: Georgetown

Climate: tropical

Population: 746,500 people

Languages: English is the official language, but you will also hear Hindi and Urdu, as well as indigenous languages: Arawak, Carib

David, Jack and Charles were all ready for their next adventure. This time they were joined by a zookeeper called Tim Vinall instead of Alf, who would set up a mini zoo in the capital Georgetown to look after the animals as they were collected.

Their plan wasn't very thought out, to say the least. They had few notes written, little transport booked and no contacts in the country like they had had in Sierra Leone. Nowadays, television programmes would require draft scripts, detailed plans of shots that they would aim to get, full costing, thorough information on both the animals and the areas they were going to, and all the permits and contacts they needed in place. However, this was 1955 and they were still working out how to do everything properly.

"IN MARCH 1955, IT SEEMED SUFFICIENT TO ME TO SAY AIRILY THAT WE WOULD BE BACK SOME TIME IN JUNE WITH, I HOPED, ENOUGH MATERIAL FOR SIX HALF-HOUR PROGRAMMES."

The partial plan they did have was that this time, rather than focusing on any single animal, they would see several different habitats in Guyana – the tropical rainforests, swampland and savannahs. And of course, find as many animals in them as possible.

Their first stop was the savannah known as the Rupununi. The area was named after the large river that runs through it and is at the south of the country. Thanks to some contacts they made in Georgetown, they were introduced to a group of people who were part of the Wapishana community, an indigenous people who live in southern Guyana. They agreed to show the film crew around and help them find some of the animals that they hoped to see in the area.

One day, some of the Wapishana invited David and the team to see them fishing using a traditional method in which they poisoned the water with the sap from lianas (a type of plant) that they gathered in the mountains. When the fish slowed down due to the poison, the people would shoot them with a bow and arrow from wooden platforms they built in the lake.

While they were filming, a woman who had been cleaning fish alerted the group to a dark hole in a nearby bank – surely some exciting beast was hiding inside?

Sneaking closer, they saw that there were two holes, one big and one small. The team had some idea what was inside and thought maybe they needed to encourage it to come out. They sealed the smaller hole with poles that had been used for fishing, and slowly began to make the other hole bigger. Jack and David crept closer, and there, in the dark of the tunnel, was a giant set of teeth. It was a black caiman – a very large reptile.

David decided he'd got quite close enough for now and retreated to the canoe Charles was filming from. As David tried to climb in, the little boat rocked and swayed in the water, and Charles almost lost the camera! David realized he was going to have to stay in the water and be very, very brave.

Meanwhile, Jack had positioned himself on the bank with a lasso in hand ready to catch the caiman. One of the most dangerous creatures in the world … and all they had was a bit of old rope. Jack leaned down, dangling the loop over the caiman's nose, and after a few attempts, he managed to hook it around its snout! The caiman, as you might imagine, was not pleased about this and let out a tremendous bellow that shook the whole bank. Determined to catch the caiman no matter the risk, Jack slid a pole down its length and managed to reach in and tie the caiman to it. Working with the Wapishana, Jack slid the giant beast out of its den.

BLACK CAIMAN

Melanosuchus niger (mell-an-o-sook-us nigh-jer)

The black caiman is a type of very large reptile, which can grow to be 5 metres long. That's as long as a parking space for a car!

They look very similar to a crocodile or an alligator, but their scales appear to be black rather than greenish-brown.

Caimans live in shallow freshwater habitats like lakes and slow-moving rivers but are also known to venture into flooded savannah land in the northern parts of South America.

While they mostly eat fish like piranhas and catfish, caimans have a varied carnivorous diet. Due to their size and strength, they can take down deer, buffalo and anacondas.

They are the largest predator in the Amazon ecosystem. They even sometimes eat people!

Like all reptiles, they are ectothermic, which means they cannot regulate their own body temperature as we mammals can. To keep themselves warm, they often sunbathe with their mouths open. Their black scales are extra effective at soaking up heat, because black as a colour absorbs all wavelengths of light and turns it into heat, making things warm.

They were hunted extensively in the 1950s–70s for their skin to make leather, but their populations have recovered and now they are considered a low conservation risk. Estimates suggest there are one million black caimans in the wild.

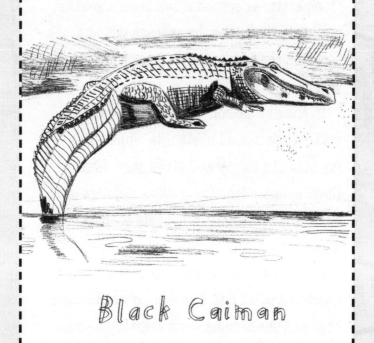

Black Caiman

TEMPERATURE-DEPENDENT SEX DETERMINATION

Did you know that black caimans can determine what sex their offspring will be based on how deep they bury the eggs? All crocodilians are able to do this. It is called "temperature-dependent sex determination", but basically means the average temperature in which the eggs incubate fixes what sex they will be.

In the dry season, female black caimans make large mound nests into which they lay between thirty and sixty eggs, where they incubate for ninety days. Reptiles (and birds and platypuses) incubate their eggs by keeping them warm while the baby reptile inside grows and develops, before it's ready to hatch out of its egg. The mound itself retains heat and the decomposing vegetation inside may also help to generate heat. At particular temperatures, genes inside the developing reptile embryo switch on to signal whether it will be male or female.

We don't know the exact temperatures for all species, but we do know that for the American alligator, 33°C signals for the eggs to develop into males, and 30°C produces females.

This process happens in all crocodilians, and some species of turtles, lizards and even some bony fish. We know that temperature does affect how many males or females will be hatched in birds, though how it happens is a little different than how we've described it here. Scientists are still exploring the ways our world affects creatures in their eggs!

After dropping off the caiman with Tim in Georgetown, their next stop was the expansive rainforest, which covers eighty-five per cent of the country. Rainforests are one of the most vibrant ecosystems in the world, filled with a huge variety of plants and animals. They flew up north to an area called the Kamarang, where they discovered some British officers had set up a station, and so made that their home base. Here they also met some Akawaio people, another indigenous people of Guyana, some of whom worked at the station where they were staying.

David was very keen to see sloths; not just the shaggy, sleepy two-toed sloths that were commonly kept in zoos, but the three-toed sloth. The three-toed sloth lives entirely on a specific type of leaf found in the rainforest, and so they are not successfully kept in captivity. Therefore, rather than collect one, they decided just to try and film one for audiences at home.

Despite how slowly they move, three-toed sloths are not very easy to find in the canopy, but after a couple of useless attempts, Jack managed to spot one high up in the trees near the airstrip. Jack had hurt his ribs and so it was up to David to clamber up the tall tree and lure the sloth on to an outstretched branch of liana plant. Up in the tree, he gently prised one sloth claw at a time off the branch, moving its paws to the liana, only for the clever sloth to move it back as soon as he turned to the next one. He kept at it, encouraging the sloth to grab on to the branch, and eventually, after much laughing from Jack and Charles at the bottom of the tree, he managed it, and brought the sloth down gently to the ground.

She was as big as a large sheepdog, with black teeth and long grey shaggy hair. They gently transferred her to a tree a little closer to their rooms, much lower down where they could easily film her. She stayed there, quite happily, munching on the particular leaves they had brought her to eat.

On the third day, they noticed a strange wet patch on her tummy. Peering closer, they realized with great surprise that it was a tiny baby sloth, which she was licking clean. She looked exhausted and hadn't eaten any of the food they'd left her overnight, so the team thought the best thing was to take her back to the tree they found her in. They lured her on to the branch they had transported her on and took her back. An hour later, mother and baby had both disappeared into the darkness of the forest.

PALE-THROATED THREE-TOED SLOTH

Bradypus tridactylus (bray-dee-puss try-dact-ee-luss)

There are six species of sloth in the world, split into two main groups – two-toed and three-toed sloths. They are found all over the northern countries of South America and live in tropical rainforest.

The sloth and her baby from Attenborough's adventure in Guyana was almost certainly a pale-throated three-toed sloth. They only eat leaves from certain trees, which makes them herbivores. Three-toed sloths are mostly nocturnal, and so usually are asleep in the day.

These hairy mammals are some of the slowest animals in the world. So slow-moving, in fact, that algae grows in their fur, often giving them a greenish tinge. Only about ten per cent of their day is spent moving at all!

Everything is done in the trees – eating, sleeping, mating and even giving birth! They use their long toe claws to hook themselves into the trees, where they can happily stay hanging, even while asleep, though sometimes they get lazy and snuggle into the fork of branches instead. Their claws and front limbs (which are fifty per cent longer than their legs) make them clumsy on land, but excellent swimmers.

One of the strangest things about them is that while most mammals have seven neck vertebrae (the thick bones that make up your spinal column), three-toed sloths may have eight or nine, which means they can rotate their heads 270 degrees!

Pale-throated Three-toed Sloth

The next day, David, Jack and Charles decided to sail upriver along the Mazaruni River with some of the Akawaio people to one of their villages, where they hoped to find lots more wildlife. The Akawaio people were master animal keepers, as hunters would often bring back the young animals they found for people in the village to raise. One of the most important things David learned during this adventure was how to care for the animals they captured. Jack would impart all sorts of wisdom about what creatures would eat or need to be happy and healthy, but they both learned a lot from the Akawaio people too.

A woman they met showed them how to feed a tiny parrot chick that they bought from her, by chewing up cassava bread (cassava is a root vegetable, a bit like a sweet potato) and pushing it out of her lips into the chick's mouth. David was initially a little squeamish but saw that the scraggly little parrot chick happily fed from her. He did the same, chewing up the bread and pushing it forward with his tongue. The chick became very excited, dancing its head about as he approached, and leaped up to David's lips to take the food. As gross as it was, David realized this was a very effective method and thanked the woman for her lesson and for the chick. This was a technique he would use again and again for feeding hatchlings while on their *Zoo Quest* expeditions. When David went to visit the parrot at the zoo some months later, the now fully-grown parrot would dance its head about whenever David called to it, perhaps remembering the cassava bread!

The team even met a pair of capybaras (the biggest of all rodents) who would only go and swim in the river with their owners' children, and would come when whistled.

The last place they visited was the swampy wetland areas near Georgetown because the animal that the zoo wanted them to bring back most of all was a manatee. They hired an extremely confident and strong fisherman called Mr King who promised he would be able to lure in a manatee for them. He described his tactic for doing this – it involved running his fingers over the net's ropes in such a way that the vibrations would soothe the manatee, and so the creature would be less likely to thrash about and could be gently tied up. (They soon realized this tactic wasn't nearly as effective as Mr King had made it out to be.)

After a few days of no sightings and assurances that the timing was not right to catch a manatee, David was getting a little suspicious and they decided to head back the way they came as they were running low on supplies. On the way, a fisherman caught up to them – he had caught a manatee only the day before and had kept it in a pond for them, just in case they had no luck! It turned out that pulling her out of the muddy pond was much more difficult than expected. Every time she rose to the surface to breathe, the men would sneak into the water to rope her but she'd either slip away at the last minute or thrash them with her gigantic paddle tail, knocking them all flying. Not even Mr King could manage it. Eventually, after a lot of trying, they managed to get a rope around her tail and haul her ashore.

WEST INDIAN MANATEE

Trichechus manatus (trih-kek-us man-at-us)

Manatees are an aquatic mammal – they live in water, but they breathe air and can remain submerged for up to twenty minutes.

They have large round bodies with thick dark skin, flippers at the front and a large paddle tail instead of back legs. They grow to around 3 metres long and can weigh up to 1,655 kg which is almost as much as a small car! They can live in both saltwater and freshwater, and they tend to live alone.

They are herbivores and graze on aquatic plants with their large lips that are covered in specialised bristles and hairs which help them to find plants and tell the difference between them. To counteract any damage to their teeth from sand, manatees constantly grow new ones and replace them throughout their life.

They are very slow-moving creatures so are vulnerable to being hit by boats, being caught in fishing nets and being hunted, and have been listed as Vulnerable on the IUCN Red List since the 1980s.

West Indian Manatee

At the end of their adventure, Charles and David flew back to London, while it was decided that Jack and Tim would come by sea with the animals. As they were preparing to leave, Jack gave David two parcels. The first was a large box containing many spiders, which he assured were all in separate little containers inside and wouldn't get out. The second was a tiny coati kitten, which he kept warm inside his shirt. South American coatis are highly social animals that look quite a lot like a raccoon, which they are closely related to, with a long, banded tail and a thin snout.

The little coati wouldn't feed on any of their long flights, rejecting every offer of milk, even when mixed up with a little cream or banana. Everyone was quite worried, but as they waited in the airport in Amsterdam for their last flight of many, Charles had a brainwave. He remembered that Jack had told them that coatis were omnivores. Perhaps the kitten might like a nice worm instead? Just outside the window, there were huge flowerbeds filled with tulips ... perhaps they would find some there? David walked outside and shuffled over to the flowerbed, hoping that no one would notice his strange behaviour. Luckily, he found several bright pink worms, which the tiny coati gobbled down happily.

Meanwhile, Jack had had to fly back to London as he became suddenly unwell, so Tim travelled back with the animals accompanied by another zookeeper from London Zoo who flew out to help. A special tank had been built for their manatee on board the ship, so that she could swim around quite happily.

Their shopping list was enormous to keep everyone fed on the nineteen-day journey home:

- 3,000 lbs of lettuce
- 100 lbs of cabbages
- 400 lbs of bananas
- 160 lbs of green grass
- 48 pineapples.

Everyone arrived back in the UK without a hitch and moved into their new home at London Zoo.

Sadly, Jack was rushed straight to hospital upon returning and passed away a short few months later. He had taught David all he knew on their two *Zoo Quest* expeditions together and had been an essential part of the exploration team. David went on to present this series once again, establishing himself as the face of *Zoo Quest*.

QUEST FOR A DRAGON

Now that they had taken viewers to Africa and South America, David decided Asia should be their next destination and that Indonesia would be the best place to start. He was very keen to film the birds of paradise that lived on a remote island, and was hopeful of seeing orangutans. There were lots of different species that they could film and that the zoo might like as well. And on top of that, there was the Komodo dragon, an enormous lizard that can be found on five Indonesian islands.

INDONESIA

Where is it: Southeast Asia

Capital: Jakarta, on the island of Java

Climate: tropical

Population: 267 million people

Languages: Bahasa Indonesia is the official language, but there are several hundred languages spoken across Indonesia.

London Zoo wouldn't send another employee in Jack's place, so David and Charles alone prepared for their third *Zoo Quest*. Thankfully, Jack had taught David a lot about caring for animals, and David sought out the advice of another explorer who knew Indonesia well, for advice on animals he'd never seen before. With only two of them, the logistics would be much more difficult, but luckily Charles was not only an excellent cameraman, but also a talented cook with good first aid knowledge.

"HE WAS THE CAMERAMAN, AND THE MEDICAL OFFICER, AND THE COOK ... AND YOU MIGHT WONDER WHAT IT IS THAT I DID. WELL, I BECAME THE CHIEF SNAKE CATCHER."

Technology had advanced far enough that this was the first series where the part filmed in the studio was recorded as well as transmitted to the public, and so the Indonesian episodes can be viewed in full to this day, with David and Charles in the studio presenting the animals they found. In 2016, an archivist working in the vaults at the BBC Natural History Unit found some old tins labelled "Zoo Quest". Inside she found colour footage from some of their expeditions, which are now available for people to see!

Adventures come with many ups and downs, but it seemed like their journey to Komodo was over before it truly began. David and Charles arrived in Jakarta in September 1957 with a letter from London Zoo explaining their mission, but it was no use whatsoever. The Indonesian government refused to grant them access to some of the islands they hoped to visit but agreed they could go to Komodo as there was nothing of importance there. (David found out some years later that British spies in Indonesia used to pretend to be bird watchers to get access to the remote islands! No wonder they didn't want him going anywhere…) This came with a condition – they could go, but they couldn't take any Komodo dragons back with them. This was a blow, as it meant the studio programme wouldn't have their main species, but they accepted this was as good as it was going to get.

However, the Surabaya Zoo suggested they employ Sabran, a trusty guide and animal catcher, whom they could find on the island of Borneo. It made sense to head there first. They arrived in Borneo in the port town of Samarinda, where they bought supplies and arranged for a boat called the *Kruwing* to take them upriver in search of animals.

Sabran

As it was hot and stuffy inside the boat, Charles and David set up mosquito-net-covered camp beds on the jetty, enjoying the fresh breeze coming off the river. The downside to this was the rats. David awoke to find a rat jumping on his mosquito net, bouncing down to just in front of his face. Half asleep and rather startled, he flung his arms out, only to realize that he'd just sent the rat flying through the air. A little splash sounded a short time later, as the rat landed in the river. Whoops!

The next time he woke was for a much more pleasant reason – Sabran had arrived. Sabran was a friendly, kind-hearted young man in his twenties, and quickly identified the animals David had drawn out on a kind of wish list, giving the local names for them. They came up with a plan to find the animals before heading off to Komodo together.

An animal that David really wanted to film was the orangutan. Along the river, they came across a group of men who informed them that an orangutan had been raiding the crops outside their village for the last few days. The men offered to guide them there but warned that the usual two-hour journey would probably take David and Charles much longer, perhaps even twice as long. David and Charles, slightly miffed, said that they were sure they could manage it. It turned out their journey was mostly through swampland, where they would walk along hidden beams, struggling for balance while their guides walked easily, despite carrying bags for them. By the time they arrived it was night, and so they camped out in the small town, surrounded by the sounds of the rainforest and the feral dogs that lived there. Needless to say, they didn't get the most restful sleep.

It took a couple of days and many unsuccessful outings for them to come across an orangutan. On the third morning, a man urgently appeared, saying that an orangutan was nearby. David, Sabran and Charles raced after him, through thorn bushes and marshy land. As they ran David lost his footing, and landed heavily on a submerged tree trunk, completely smashing his binoculars and giving his ribs a good whack. Stumbling to his feet, determined not to miss out, he saw his guide pointing up.

There, in the tree above them, was a male orangutan. He was not very happy to see them and kept throwing branches down. Charles decided to film him for just a little while as they'd come such a long way. As they turned to leave, a gunshot rang out. One of the men who'd accompanied them there had shot at the orangutan, and fortunately missed. David asked him why he would do such a thing, to which the man simply said that it was eating all his food. David realized that animals that appear mysterious and beautiful to us may cause many problems for the people that have to live alongside them.

BORNEAN ORANGUTAN

Pongo pygmaeus (pon-goh pig-may-us)

There are three species of orangutan across Sumatra and Borneo. The name orangutan means "man of the forest", because they can look like old men wearing capes with their shaggy hair. The orangutans that

David met in Borneo were of course Bornean orangutans.

Orangutans have dark brown or tanned skin covered with coarse bright red hair. You can easily tell the adult males apart from the females by looking at their flat bald cheek pads on the side of their head, which make their whole head look much bigger. Males are also usually twice as large as females and can be 1.2 metres (4 feet) tall – that's probably as tall as you are now!

They have very long arms (proportionally much, much longer than yours) and short legs, which makes sense for a creature that spends ninety per cent of its time awake in the trees.

Orangutans make sleeping platforms by weaving together twigs and broken branches. They also make similar structures to protect them from the rain, a kind of leafy umbrella.

Orangutans are semi-solitary which means most of the time they live alone, unlike other great apes such as chimpanzees, gorillas and humans, or even monkeys. Usually you'd only find five or six adults living in a square mile.

While they love ripe fruit – particularly the very smelly durian fruit – they eat over 400 different types of food. A very varied diet! A little meat, some leaves, the occasional bug. Delicious!

Orangutans have the longest gap between babies of all mammals. They are pregnant for nine months, just like humans. After giving birth, they might wait another eight years or so before having another baby. This means that their population grows very, very slowly.

The Bornean and Sumatran orangutans are listed as critically endangered species, as they are both under threat from hunting, and habitat loss because of farming and logging.

Orangutan

This lone male wasn't the only orangutan that David and Charles would come across on the island of Borneo. A few days later, they sailed further along the river to meet with a hunter that Sabran knew would occasionally catch animals and sell them on.

When they arrived, the hunter told them that he had killed an orangutan that had been raiding his crops, and, as a result of this action, found and caught an orphaned baby, perhaps only two years old. Sabran bargained with the hunter, trading salt and tobacco for the young and very frightened orangutan.

Back on the *Kruwing*, they transferred the orangutan to a larger cage, and let him be for much of the next two days so that he could recover. Charlie, as they named him, was frightened by David, but it turned out he quite liked condensed milk, which is thick and very sweet.

Over a few days, Charlie grew in confidence every time David brought him a treat, and even let David touch him. David quickly realized that Charlie had sustained some wounds from the hunter, and gently applied antiseptic cream to them while Charlie lapped up the milk. After this, Charlie quickly bonded with David, reaching out to grab David's hand every time he passed his cage.

In no time at all, Charlie had settled happily on the boat and would roam around, often sitting at the front of the boat with the driver, happily munching on a raw egg.

Charlie turned out to be an incredibly important member of London Zoo. He was the father of the first orangutan to be born in Britain at London Zoo, and thus kick-started their orangutan captive breeding programme. David visited Charlie regularly at the zoo for the rest of his life.

Charlie wasn't the only orphaned baby that David brought home from Borneo. Benjamin, a tiny sun bear, was brought to him by a young man who found the animal alone in the forest.

SUN BEARS

Helarctos malayanus (hell-arc-toss mal-aye-an-us)

Sun bears are found throughout Southeast Asia, and are jet black with light orange fur around their snout and eyes, and a bright orange or yellow deep V shape on their chest.

They are the smallest bear species, and they don't hibernate like other bears do. Their favourite foods are bees, honey and even beehives themselves, but they also eat a mixture of insects and fruit, including the very smelly durian fruit.

David reckoned the cub must only have been about two weeks old and was covered in little maggots. He quickly fed him up on warm milk from a bottle every three hours. Benjamin made a funny screeching noise whenever he was hungry and wanted a bottle.

When they eventually returned to London, Benjamin was still too young to go to the zoo as he was feeding regularly from a bottle, so Charles decided to take him home, where Benjamin terrorized Charles's dog and ripped up the curtains. Once Benjamin was a little older, and much, much bigger, he went to live at London Zoo.

The journey from Borneo to Komodo was going to be much more difficult, and all the direct options meant waiting weeks. In the end they took a circuitous route by air to Maumere, the main town on the island of Flores, which was as close to Komodo as they were going to get, hoping to find a boat when they got there. As the plane touched down, the pilot warned that he would be immediately flying back as the rainy season was starting and he was about to tell the airlines that no more planes should land here, as it was getting too wet and dangerous. David realized they were not only going to have to find a boat to Komodo, but also find one to take them back to Jakarta for their plane home.

Luckily, after asking around for a while, they

were introduced to a surly captain of the only fishing boat, or *prau*, left in the harbour. Sabran explained that they needed to get to Komodo, and the captain agreed, for a hefty price. The *prau* itself was a small boat made of wood and bamboo, only about 6 metres long, with a single mast topped with a small sail – not much space for four adult men and the two young boys who came along to steer the boat. The cabin hold, where they stored their bags, was tiny and smelled of rotten fish, so David and Charles decided to risk sleeping on deck to avoid the horrible stink. Compared to this, the *Kruwing* had been a luxury vessel. It would turn out that the cabin wasn't the only thing that stank.

As they set off around the coast of Flores towards Komodo, the tiny boat ran aground on a coral reef! The captain seemed unbothered and, after taking his time to get up, used a long pole to push them off the coral. This seemed worrying to David. Most captains didn't run aground on coral so easily, especially if they knew the way...

The second day they awoke to find completely still waters and no wind. The boat didn't have an engine and relied on wind, and without it they simply floated about in the water, going nowhere. They ended up stranded in pretty much the same spot for three days! Can you imagine sitting on a tiny boat with nowhere to go for three days? The drudgery was only broken by a pod of dolphins that passed by the boat one afternoon for a few minutes.

David and Charles were not used to eating just plain rice for dinner and asked the captain to catch some fish for them. It turned out the captain was not a fisher and had brought no lines to catch food for them to eat either. David was even more suspicious. Who was this man? That night, the fourth night at sea, David felt a gentle breeze against his skin. Maybe the wind was finally picking up? He asked the captain how long it was to sail to Komodo from where they were, at which point the captain slowly responded that he did not know as he had never been there before, and didn't have a map.

David, Charles and Sabran realized with horror that they were confined to a tiny boat with someone who had absolutely no intention of helping them get anywhere. The only maps David had brought were a detailed one of Komodo itself, and an airline map that showed Indonesia as a whole, on which Komodo was merely a dot. All they could do was tell the captain to head south in the direction they thought Komodo might be, and hope.

It soon became very obvious they were caught in a strong current that ran between the chain of islands. The channel was filled with whirlpools, which dragged and tugged at their tiny boat, threatening to capsize them. As they escaped one whirlpool, they would be dragged straight into another one, or hurled forward by a strong tidal current, or thrown perilously close to a sharp-looking coral reef. It took many hours of careful steering, quick thinking and hope, but they finally arrived safely in Komodo Bay. They slept on the boat, exhausted and relieved to have got this far unscathed.

The next morning, they visited the large village at the bay to ask about the dragons. The head of the town told them there were many Komodo dragons on the island, and where to find them, but warned them that the dragons had a keen sense of smell and were dangerous. He also added that they were not as good to eat as the island pigs, so people didn't hunt them much, and that the dragons sometimes came into the village, attracted by their rubbish tips. Much like foxes in the UK. David thanked him for all this extremely useful information and bought from him two slaughtered goats so they could try to attract a dragon the next day.

The next morning, they walked inland for an hour to an area where the Komodo dragons had been seen before, near the dry gravelly bed of what was sometimes a stream. The goat carcasses they had brought with them certainly smelt quite ripe, and they began to make a large boxed enclosure to lure the dragon into and trap it.

Sabran had built enclosures like these before to capture leopards, with a door that would drop down when the animal takes the bait. While the government of Indonesia had said they couldn't take any dragons away with them, they could trap them to get a closer look and some footage. They returned the next day to find footprints around the trap but no dragon inside. The dragon was much smarter than they had planned for.

Ever determined, David dragged one of the goat carcasses out of the trap and lay it in the middle of the dried-out stream. He, Charles and Sabran retreated behind a bush to wait.

Half an hour later, David heard a rustle behind them. Perhaps someone had come to join them? He slowly turned around and saw, only a few metres away, a ten-foot-long Komodo dragon, with dark skin and beady eyes watching them. Charles quietly changed the lens on his camera, which suddenly let out a loud whirr! But the dragon didn't stir and stood as if waiting. As they watched, a butterfly landed on its nose.

Suddenly, a cry sounded near the bait, and they saw two other dragons heading towards the goat. The first one followed, and the three giant lizards tore into the meat, as Charles filmed.

David decided now was the time to be brave and take some photographs, but his camera lens was not good enough to take long-range photos. He would have to get closer. He inched forward slowly, closer and closer.

The dragons barely seemed to notice. He was so close that the toes of his boots were almost touching the carcass. It was only when Charles and Sabran appeared from behind the bush that the dragons, perhaps realizing they were now equally matched in number, scuttled off.

Determined to get some more footage, David hung the goat up in a tree to try and lure them closer to the trap, and retreated behind the bush again. It quickly became clear that he had underestimated how tall the largest dragon was, because when it returned, it stood on its hind legs and quickly wolfed down the rest of the bait. As it turned to leave, the smell of the meat in the trap must have caught its attention, as it slowly wandered over ... and straight into it, the door slamming shut behind it. David, Charles and Sabran ran over excitedly, taking more photographs and filming close-ups of the dragon, before quietly backing away and releasing it. They had completed their quest for the dragon.

Back at the village that night, the head of the village warned them that the captain they had hired wasn't only useless but he was plotting to rob David and Charles, and had been trying to get more people from Komodo to join him. The head assured them that no one would. The group nervously returned to and boarded the boat, encouraging the captain to take them a few islands over to where they knew there was an airstrip. Then, they paid him off and escaped with everything.

In the 1980s, David returned to Komodo to film the dragons again for *The Living Planet*, hoping to get some footage in colour. The island was very, very different. There were now regularly chartered tourist boats, and erected platforms to stand on to watch Komodo dragons feeding, as well as many signs instructing you not to approach the creatures. Getting close enough to film them without also including tourists was quite difficult, and David felt a little sad. He knew that publicising the dragons had somewhat contributed to this tourism, but was pleased the money earned from people visiting them would go to their conservation. We call this ecotourism, and it is a very popular way of funding conservation now.

KOMODO DRAGONS

Varanus komodoensis (var-an-us ko-mo-doh-en-sis)

Komodo dragons are large reptiles related to monitor lizards, and not really dragons, though the name sounds pretty good. They have thick muscular tails, very long and sharp claws, tough skin and extremely sharp eyesight. They can grow to be over 3 metres (almost 10 feet) long!

They live almost exclusively on Komodo island in Indonesia but have been found on some other islands. We know they get around these islands by swimming, which they are very good at, but haven't explored further into Indonesia because many of these islands are surrounded by open ocean with strong currents and very deep channels, which the dragons cannot swim across.

They are the top predator in their habitat and they are carnivorous – this means they only consume meat, eating a variety of birds, large mammals and other reptiles. They have a powerful bite with serrated teeth.

The worst part about being bitten by a Komodo dragon is that they produce venom in their mouths –this is released from ducts between their teeth, which they can then force into their prey's bloodstream. Everyone used to think it was just some kind of horrible flesh-eating bacteria, but nope, it's venom. Overall, pretty ferocious!

Komodo dragon

In 2006, a pair of Komodo dragons were brought to live in Chester Zoo. After a few days, the female, Flora, laid some eggs. Everyone was a little surprised because the male and female had been kept separately in their own enclosures to make sure they didn't fight. The keepers decided that she must have got pregnant before her journey to Chester and were pleased to see a group of Komodo babies. Except, only a few months later, it happened again. The keepers were stumped!

They checked the enclosures to make sure there was no way they could reach each other. They suspected something truly special was happening and contacted scientists at the University of Liverpool to look at the DNA of the babies. The clever scientists discovered that the babies were all clones of Flora. This means that she passed on 100 per cent of her genes and that she was, in a sense, both parents to her babies. This is called asexual reproduction or parthenogenesis and was the first time it had ever been witnessed in Komodo dragons.

JANE AND THE BABIES

David was able to go off on these long expeditions thanks to the support of his wife, Jane, who stayed home and raised their children, Robert and Susan. Because of this, David was able to produce phenomenal documentaries and bring nature to the viewing public.

Additionally, it turns out that Jane played an even bigger role with the animals, as she was particularly good at caring for them.

David had always kept a wide range of creatures since he was a small boy and, shortly after they married, he convinced Jane that spending some of his tiny publishing salary on a large fish tank was a good investment.

Every time he returned from a trip, the animal menagerie in their Richmond home grew a little more. Cockatoos, aquariums of fish, lemurs, monkeys and a small colony of bush babies – who eventually had their own babies, which the Attenboroughs gave to the zoo – were all looked after by Jane while David travelled.

Jane became so well known and admired for her excellent care and understanding that zookeepers from London Zoo would often ask her for advice, especially with sick animals.

Once, a tiny gibbon baby that needed round-the-clock care, else he might die, was brought to Jane. Jane, knowing immediately what he needed, popped him in a sling and carried him wherever she went. Sammy, as she named him, would howl if she left him alone for too long. He also had quite a rude habit of interrupting telephone conversations with a very loud burp.

The last *Zoo Quest* programme focused on Australia. It was called *Quest Under Capricorn* and aired in 1963, though it featured no capturing of animals at all. The idea of collecting animals from the wild was starting to look dated and instead zoos were turning to the challenge and exploration of breeding programmes.

Meanwhile, David decided to explore a different career. At the start of the 1960s, he resigned from being permanent staff at the BBC and went to study social anthropology at a university in London, in between his last *Zoo Quest* programmes.

But before he could finish his degree, he was offered an exciting new job in TV – running their second-ever channel, BBC Two. The BBC had been experimenting for years with new technologies, including colour, and had decided to transmit a second channel on 625 lines on an ultra-high frequency band, instead of the 405-line technology they were currently using.. It would start in black and white and then move to colour in the future.

This decision caused a huge change in structures – totally new transmitters had to be built, along with new studios, and the government (whose idea it was) said it all had to be done as soon as possible.

Michael Peacock initially took on the role later offered to David, but there was an uphill struggle with the sudden need to commission new programmes and ensure they had the studios to film them. Also, it turned out to be quite challenging persuading viewers to switch over to the second channel – the few people who'd invested in this new technology so they could watch BBC Two were less than pleased and ratings were disappointing. Not too long after it started, David got a call. Perhaps he would take the job as head of the channel instead?

This was very different from his plan of becoming an anthropologist and he would have to give up his studies to do it. But, he had a young family at home, with two children, and the stability of a proper job was tempting. This new job also meant creating a whole new type of television, which David couldn't refuse. He would be able to commission totally new programmes with a virtually empty schedule to fill (as most of the previous programmes would be scrapped), and its audience was very small, so things really could only get better. For a TV man, it was truly exciting. (Somewhat ironically, David's son Robert is a lecturer in anthropology!)

"EVERYBODY FORGOT I WASN'T JUST A NATURALIST — I WAS ALWAYS A TRAINED TV MAN. HELL, I LOVE IT. I WATCH EVERYTHING. STRAIGHT HOME FROM THE OFFICE — SWITCH TO BBC TWO — SEE ALL MY BABIES."

He agreed to it, on the condition that every eighteen months he could go off and make a documentary in order to keep him interested and up to date with the latest filming technology.

The BBC agreed. He started the job at the beginning of March in 1965. Thanks to the new colour technology, snooker matches were now much more popular, along with cricket and rugby league highlights.

He also commissioned a range of comedy shows, and in 1972 championed what was known as "community programming", where minority or marginalized groups could suggest ideas for factual programmes based on their activities or interests.

LIFE ON EARTH

hile David was working as controller for BBC2, the BBC's Natural History Department had been thinking of developing a detailed series about the world. It would be like some of the successful historical and anthropological shows that David had commissioned. These would be in-depth series and would take a few years to film.

By 1972, David realized he was fed up with sitting at a desk. He resigned from the job, deciding to become a freelance producer of natural history films intended for the BBC – this would give him much more freedom and meant very little desk time. The Natural History Department got in touch and asked him if he would be interested in making an in-depth series of his own. The scope of the programme would be the development and evolution of life. They quickly realized it would be very expensive to make and so the BBC producers had to go to an American network to get them to co-fund the programme.

While waiting to get started on this new series, David did a couple of short programmes about indigenous people around the world and the animals in the countries where they lived. No longer was he filmed hiding behind trees or in the studio showing animals they had caught. Now there were scripts, and producers also wanted David on camera to react to things he saw, as well as describe the environment and relay a few facts. It was much more about presenting than exploration.

By 1976, they had the money, the staff and the plans, and David and his team got to work. *Life on Earth* would be a thirteen-part series, in which they would show the evolution of life using both fossils and living creatures across the world. Each episode would explore a different group of animals or stage in evolutionary time, taking the viewer from the first simple single-celled creatures all the way to humans.

While David planned, narrated and presented the series, there was a team of six camera operators working over the three years in different parts of the world. They also hired sixteen specialist camera operators for specific shots.

"NOW I JUST WRITE AND SPEAK THE WORDS ... THIRTY CAMERAMEN WORKED ON THIS THING." I'M GIVEN CREDIT FOR THINGS I DON'T DO. I AM GRATEFUL, BUT I'M ALSO EMBARRASSED."

David would travel around with a small team like in the *Zoo Quest* days for the shots that would include him, while other small teams would focus on filming the other shots required. It was not possible to film everything in the order that it was shown as they jumped around between countries a lot, so they arranged to film the shots David was in into groups allowing them to film parts of many episodes in one go. David would sometimes even finish a sentence of a narration he began in one place several years later on a completely different continent.

One of the most difficult things to record was a tiny green male frog, who carried eggs in its vocal sack, where they would hatch. The hard part was timing it, waiting for the moment the little frogs would clamber out. The cameraman and his assistant waited for 140 hours!

To show the variety of life, it was important that they travelled to many different countries and climates. One of the most important places David travelled to was the Galapagos Islands.

The Galapagos Islands are a group of nineteen islands and many islets in the Pacific Ocean, 600 miles west of Ecuador. They are known for their periodically active volcanos and unique plants and animals. The islands have been under protection for much of the last 100 years to preserve biodiversity: in 1934 certain parts of the island were designated as wildlife sanctuaries by the government of Ecuador; in 1959 a new law was introduced that declared all the islands a national park (rather than just certain parts); in 1978 the islands were declared a UNESCO World Heritage Site; and in 1986 this was extended beyond the islands themselves, to the waters, to create a marine reserve. As a result, only three per cent of the Galapagos is inhabited by humans – the remaining ninety-seven per cent is a national park.

GALAPAGOS ISLANDS

Where is it? Pacific Ocean, 600 miles west of Ecuador

Capital: Puerto Baquerizo Moreno on San Cristóbal island

Climate: subtropical – low rainfall, low humidity, and low temperatures

Population: 25,000 people

Languages: Spanish

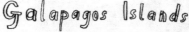

In the sixteenth century, the islands were used as important bases by pirates, as well as whale and seal hunters. Possibly the most famous visitor to the Galapagos Islands was Charles Darwin, as his discoveries there would change the way we view nature and science for ever.

CHARLES DARWIN

Charles Darwin was an English adventurer and naturalist, who travelled the world looking at animals and plants.

At university in Edinburgh, he first learned of the idea that simple invertebrates (animals without a spine) may hold the key to understanding the origins of complex animals, and focused on studying marine invertebrates.

His father wanted him to work in the Church and didn't approve of his studies, so sent Darwin to Cambridge to prepare for a life as a clergyman.

Darwin was a religious man, but this career wasn't the one for him. His fascination with nature couldn't be deterred, and after reading naturalist and explorer Alexander von Humboldt's account of exploring South America, he decided he would do the same.

He famously travelled around the world in the 1830s on the HMS *Beagle*, starting in England, travelling to South America, across the Pacific and around the south of Australia, across the Indian Ocean and around the tip of Africa, back to London.

When he reached the volcanic Galapagos, Darwin started to solidify his ideas about how animals came to be. There he saw animals that were similar to those that he'd seen on the mainland of Ecuador, but just slightly different. A type of bird resembled the cormorants he'd seen, but these had stunted wings so they couldn't fly. He also found iguanas that swam in the sea, which was very unusual (more on them later!). Once he came across the giant tortoises, he began to form ideas that would become his theory of evolution (don't worry, we'll explain this!), which he would eventually publish in his book *On the Origin of Species*.

Like the iguanas and cormorants, the tortoises were a little different from those on the mainland – they were many times bigger! As Darwin travelled around the nineteen islands, he discovered some notable differences between the tortoises and that there were two distinct shapes to their shells.

On the islands where the land was dryer with few plants, the tortoises had to reach up to get leaves from trees or to eat cactuses. Their shells had a raised part at the front, a small peak like the front of a saddle for a horse. This shape made it easy for them to lift their very long necks and heads high.

Meanwhile, on lush islands with lots of vegetation lower down, the tortoises didn't have this at all, and their shells were dome-shaped. Darwin realized that these tortoises, who had perhaps once all been the same species, had gradually changed to suit the vegetation available on their islands. This is called **"natural selection"**.

NATURAL SELECTION AND EVOLUTION

To understand evolution, we first have to understand how a species can change over time. In humans, when the two parents' DNA is combined to make offspring, sometimes the offspring is born with a new characteristic that neither of the parents have. This is called a **"mutation"** and happens completely at random. Sometimes these differences can give the offspring an advantage in life and a better chance at survival.

For example:

1. Imagine you are an animal born with extremely good hearing, better than even your parents'. This is most likely because one of your genes mutated in a way that made your ears super sensitive.

2. Your excellent hearing means you can easily locate drinking water, as your hearing abilities allow you to make out the bubbling sounds of nearby rivers, and you can hear predators or prey long before anyone else. Other members of your species that can't hear as well are therefore more likely to be caught and eaten by predators.

3. The advantages that come with this mean you'd be more likely to produce healthy offspring; possibly even with your gene that allows excellent hearing.

4. This will allow your offspring to benefit in the same way you did, and as a result they will probably grow up healthy and produce offspring too, also passing on their excellent hearing ability. Now, the mutated gene that provided you with excellent hearing will be passed on from generation to generation.

This ability to survive and thrive because of your good genes, which are then passed on to your children, is called **"natural selection"**.

Over time, all your descendants might have excellent hearing. Meanwhile, all the animals with weaker hearing might have been eaten or died out before they could have offspring – meaning that their genes would not have been passed on to new generations. Eventually, all the members of your species might have this improved hearing. This longer process is called **"evolution"**.

Lots of small changes, like improved hearing or larger paws, can add up over time, meaning that members of your species might look completely different as time goes on. Eventually these animals might change so much that they are even considered an entirely new species.

For a programme about evolution, David wanted to go and see these giant tortoises that Darwin had stumbled across many years before. Not least of all because they'd be relatively straightforward to film, as their relaxed speed would make it easy to get close-ups. To get to the tortoises' habitat, however, David would have to climb a volcano.

GALAPAGOS GIANT TORTOISE
Chelonidis nigra (kee-lon-oy-diss nie-gra)

Each of these different island populations of tortoises belong to one big group of species we call the Galapagos Giant Tortoise. Scientists have looked at the genes of these island populations and concluded that they are very, very closely related, but there are still lots of ongoing arguments about whether they are all individual species or not.

There were around fifteen species originally, but now there are only eleven species left, as four have become extinct. In fact, one of them on the island of Fernandina was thought to be extinct, but a very old female, possibly over one hundred years old, was found on the island in 2009.

There are around 20,000 individual Galapagos giant tortoises left in the wild. Only one species of saddle-backed giant tortoises lived on Isabela Island, where David and the team planned to visit. The largest population lived in a remote part the island, inside a big crater of an extinct volcano called Alcedo – which also gave them their name, the Alcedo giant tortoise.

David and the team – Maurice Fisher and Hugh Maynard on camera, Dickie Bird on sound – set out to find them. It took them two whole days to climb the volcano over roasting-hot black volcanic rock, carrying all their camera gear and enough supplies to keep them going. They had to carry two gallons of drinking water per person to make sure no one got dehydrated.

On the second day, they reached the crater

rim at 1,128 metres (3,700 feet) high – that's taller than Snowdon, the tallest mountain in Wales!

As they descended into the crater, they came across about two hundred tortoises. They set up camp quickly and got to work filming. The tortoises didn't seem to mind the men to begin with, but if David and his crew got too close, the tortoises would hiss loudly and retract their limbs into their shells. Tortoises were wandering around, eating, snoozing with their necks stretched out, and sitting in puddles. Giant tortoises are known to spend around sixteen hours a day resting and are so sedentary that small birds often perch on top of them, pecking off any ticks that might nibble at the tortoise's skin.

But some tortoises were unusually active. It was mating season, quite a noisy business for the tortoises, with the males stomping about, fighting with each other and roaring the entire time. The whole thing can go on for several hours. Once a male has picked a suitable female, they waddle after her. Once they mate, the female lays between two and sixteen tennis-ball-sized eggs in a hole, where they bury them and leave them to develop under the sun.

That afternoon it began to rain, so the group returned to camp. Unfortunately, while they had been busy filming, a few tortoises had mistaken their tents for female tortoises and completely flattened them. Needless to say, their night in damp, broken tents was not the best sleep they'd ever had.

WHAT ARE FOSSILS?

Did you know that we are aware that evolution exists because of fossils? Fossils are evidence of animals or plants from the past, which have been preserved over time and can be viewed today. This evidence might be their remains (shells, bones, exoskeletons) or imprints, like footsteps or the shape of animals' bodies.

One way that an animal or plant can be fossilised is by the remains being buried. This slows down the process of decomposition or breaking down and stops scavenging animals from eating them. They would also need to have hard parts capable of being fossilised.

Sometimes soft tissues (like muscles, skin or even feathers) can be preserved quickly if they are buried very soon after the animal or plant dies. These soft tissues turn to stone in a process called "petrification". However, most soft tissues do not get preserved well enough for us to see them in detail.

The exception to this is when a creature or plant is preserved in amber. Amber is a transparent, golden lump of fossilised tree sap. When trees are damaged they leak sticky sap that sometimes traps insects, which then die. These insects are then for ever preserved in the sap, looking pretty much the same as they did on the day they became stuck. A bit of a gruesome way to go!

FOSSILS AND EVOLUTION

Our entire knowledge of fossils found over the world and how they are dated is called the "fossil record" – this is how we know which time period some species of animals or plants appeared, died out or began to change.

The oldest fossils in the world are many billions of years old!

We can find out the age of the rock in which a fossil is found using a technique called "radiometric dating", which looks for radioactive atoms that are naturally trapped inside rocks as they form. These atoms slowly break down, and they do so in a way that allows us to learn a lot about them.

By looking at how degraded the atoms are, in either the same rock the fossil was in or other rocks around it, we can estimate how long they have been trapped inside, and therefore how old the rock is.

There are two famous types of animals that fossilised well and are often found in rocks – trilobites and ammonites. David decided that it was not only important to show these fossilised animals but their close descendants that still live today, and how they are similar and different from each other. These creatures are sometimes called "living fossils", which is a bit of a confusing name but basically means they are quite ancient in terms of their body structure and habits, and have not changed much over history.

TRILOBITES

Trilobites are a type of fossilised creature that look a little like a woodlouse. They were very common marine animals and first appeared in the Cambrian Period, about 542 million years ago. Their bodies are split up into lots of segments, and each segment has a pair of legs attached. They are a type of arthropod, a group of animals that includes spiders, insects and crustaceans such as lobsters. Like the arthropods we see today, trilobites had a hard external skeleton, called an exoskeleton, made of a material called chitin, which fossilised well. Most species of trilobites had compound eyes, which are the type of bulbous eyes you see on flies, made up of lots of tiny cells that distinguish light and colour.

One of their closest relatives that still lives today is a peculiar creature called the horseshoe crab. Despite its name, it's not really a type of crab and is more closely related to spiders and scorpions!

Like their ancestors the trilobites, they have segmented bodies but it's harder to tell because of their enormous dome-shaped shell, called a "cephalothorax", which covers their whole body.

Their shells have small spikes on them, especially in the back half, and a long sharp-looking tail. They have tiny compound eyes peeking out the top of their shells. Horseshoe crabs tend to live in estuarine waters, where rivers meet the sea, and can grow to be just over half a metre long!

There are several species of horseshoe crabs, but the most well known is the American species – *Limulus polyphemus* (lim-you-luss polly-fee-muss), which is the species David Attenborough set out to film.

Determined to feature horseshoe crabs in his early episodes of *Life on Earth*, David headed for a beach in New Jersey, USA, where they were known to appear. One of the programme's researchers told David that on 1 June 1977, as the sun was setting, they would find many horseshoe crabs. David decided that was when he would visit, and hoped that this information was accurate – before the Internet and mobile phones, it was much harder to get answers quickly!

The crew arrived in the early afternoon, but there were no horseshoe crabs, just a lot of gulls and wading birds hanging around as if waiting for something. As the sun sank, horseshoe crabs began to emerge from the water, more and more appearing and scuttling along the sand. The researcher was right – that day turned out to have the highest nocturnal tide of the year for that specific beach. It was a mass spawning: the one night of the year where horseshoe crabs all group together on a beach to mate.

One of the most fascinating things that we have learned about horseshoe crabs since *Life on Earth* is that their blood is very different from ours, in a way that has been useful for medical science. In our blood, we have a molecule called haemoglobin, which carries the oxygen we breathe in from the air around our bodies and makes our blood look red. Horseshoe crabs have a totally different chemical for carrying oxygen which makes their blood bright blue.

Their blood also contains a clever protein that clots the blood when it comes into contact with bacteria, or chemicals called "endotoxins" which are released by bacteria. Bacteria and endotoxins can make people very unwell and so a test was developed using horseshoe-crab blood to check for bacteria on medical instruments like pacemakers, joint replacements and even vaccines. The horseshoe crabs are collected from the wild, a sample of blood is taken from them and then they are released again within twenty-four hours. Who'd have thought that one of our most ancient creatures could be so important for advances in medical science?

The other fossilised creature that David focused on was the ammonite.

AMMONITES

As with the trilobite, ammonites are a group of several species that look very similar – it's impossible to tell if two fossilised creatures that look similar are indeed of the same species when you can't simply check their DNA.

Ammonites were cephalopods, which are a group of marine animals including octopus, squid and cuttlefish. They had a signature spiral shell made of coils called whorls, with clearly separated chambers called septa that you can see easily on a cross section or imprint fossil. The septa all had frilled edges, running through the whole shell, visible on the outside too.

The ammonite itself only lived in the last chamber in the centre, while all the others were filled with air or water so that the ammonite could change its buoyancy (how floaty it is) and which direction it moved in, like a submarine does! The shell also protected them and often was covered with spines and knobs to deter predators from attacking them.

They are important fossils because they are found all over the world in what scientists believe were once shallow seas. Their closest relative currently alive today is the argonaut.

Unfortunately, argonauts are vulnerable to ocean acidification, which is a side effect of climate change – the acidic waters degrade their calcium shells. (We'll learn a bit more about this later in the book.)

The final ancient animal that David was determined to film was the coelacanth (see-luh-kanth). These are a primitive-looking type of fish that for a very long time were thought to have become extinct along with the dinosaurs. But why is a fish so special? Well, to explain that we have to look at how vertebrate animals evolved.

VERTEBRATE ANIMALS AND THE COELACANTH

Vertebrate animals are those with bones, like you and me. The first vertebrates were a type of fish, something like a prehistoric shark.

Different species of fish evolved from this ancestor fish – we call this group of species "ray-finned fish". This is because they have bony parts to their fins. Salmon, swordfish, seahorses and even eels are types of ray-finned fish – they are a big group with lots of different-looking fish!

But what came next? After these bony fish, along came the ancestors of amphibians: in between fish and amphibians were a group of animals that were a mix of the two. They were animals that walked on land as well as living in the sea. They lived in the water but had skeletons more like a four-legged animal's. We call these species "transitional forms".

One of these early species was a coelacanth. These huge fish have been around for 350 million years and were found all over the world. But what makes them so special?

Their pair of fleshy lobe fins at the front look a little like legs with fins instead of toes. These fins are quite thick, unlike the usual fins you might think of on a goldfish. Coelacanths use these fleshy fins to clamber about on the rocky seafloor on which they live, while their back fins help them swim about. Scientists think that these limbs, somewhere between a fin and a leg, look a lot like those that first took animals out of the sea and on to the land.

The first living coelacanth in years was netted in the Indian Ocean in 1938 by a fisher who was so surprised by the discovery that he called museum official Marjorie Courtenay-Latimer to come and look at it. Marjorie researched this strange creature, even though her colleagues told her it was just a big cod. An ichthyologist (fish scientist) friend, Professor J.L.B. Smith, alerted her that she had one of the most important finds of the twentieth century – a living example of a species long thought extinct. All they needed was another fish to confirm their findings. Another was found in 1952 in the Comoros Islands, north of Madagascar. It turned out that the people of the Comoros knew the coelacanth fish very well, and often dried them out to eat! And so, thanks to Marjorie Courtenay-Latimer's determination, the coelacanth became un-extinct.

There are two species of coelacanth; one in Indonesia and this African one, called West Indian Ocean coelacanth – *Latimeria chalumnae* (lat-ee-mer-ee-ah cal-um-nay). These fish live deep in the open ocean, in the mesopelagic zone, which means between 200 and 1,000 metres below the surface. Only one per cent of light reaches down to this murky zone of the sea. This would be a huge filming challenge.

coelacanth fish

David and his expert underwater cameraman, Peter Scoones, attached a baited underwater camera to a very long cable and lowered it down from the boat they were on, into the gloomy depths. On the first night of filming, they drove the boat out to a patch of sea that was deep enough for them to potentially film a coelacanth. As they gently lowered the camera, they realized that the current was incredibly strong. It was too deep for them to anchor the boat, so they were dragged slowly along, towing the camera, which was transmitting some quite murky pictures of the seafloor some 200 metres (656 feet) below them.

They tried filming for several nights, but on the fifth night, disaster struck! On the monitor, David spied an enormous rocky reef. They ran to the cable and began hauling as quickly as they could, but suddenly on the screen there was a flash, zig-zag lines, and then nothing. The camera had got caught on the reef and snapped free. And they hadn't found a coelacanth at all. Luckily, a kind villager allowed David to borrow one of her dried coelacanths to use for the programme, which would have to do.

A little glum, David left the Comoros Islands to continue filming the series, but Peter stayed behind to get some more footage of the fruit bats and lemurs they had been filming in between boat trips. The day after David left, a fisherman sent for Peter to come down to the docks. He had caught a coelacanth! At the docks, they released the fish into the harbour to film it. The coelacanth was very weak, having been brought up from 300 metres down, but they managed to film it swimming around a little bit. It was the first time a living coelacanth had ever been filmed for TV.

David also managed to find the next step in the evolutionary story for the programme. The coelacanths had the first step in developing legs, but what about breathing? Fish use oxygen in the water to breathe through their gills, but to take it from air requires a different set of organs. David travelled back to East Africa in the dry season to locate a particular animal. He marched out on to a savannah plain, armed with a spade, and began digging into some dry, caked ground that used to be a pond. After a moment, David found a big clump of mud with a little fish snout sticking out of it. Inside was an air-breathing fish.

LUNGFISH

Lungfish have a long pouch in their stomachs lined with blood vessels that can absorb oxygen through its lining. They suck air in through their mouths, which sometimes makes a funny noise.

As the rainy season ends, the water evaporates and their ponds dry up, the fish bury themselves in the soft mud at the bottom. As the water continues to evaporate, they make themselves a cocoon to sleep in, go into a deep sleep and the mud eventually solidifies around them. The fish wake up when the rains return and wash away their mud cocoon.

David recreated this event by gently lowering the mud clod into a tank of water. The soil and dirt slowly crumbled away, showing a papery cocoon of dried mucous around the fish – that's like making a little bed for yourself out of snot! Gross, huh? As the cocoon fell away and the fish awoke, it swam to the surface and took a very deep breath – it was still used to breathing air, not water, and it takes a little while for them to swap over.

If one animal had these fleshy legs and this air-breathing stomach, then they could be the first fish that successfully lived on land. We have seen some fossilised fish that have both of these characteristics. They spent more and more time on land and bridged the gap between fish and amphibians.

WHAT'S IN
YOUR TOOLBOX?

Having looked at the way physical bodies have changed, David wanted to look at how behaviour is also a key part of evolution.

One of the most interesting examples of this is the use of tools. Not many animals can use tools, but the behaviour can be seen in several different species of animals that aren't closely related to each other – certain species of sea urchins, insects, spiders, octopus, fish, birds and mammals have all been shown to use tools. This means that the behaviour has evolved independently in each of these species.

To be able to use a tool an animal has to have a very nimble beak, claws or fingers. Tool use may be seen across the whole species, or it might be a local adaptation to a habitat seen in only one population. Sea otters will use small rocks to smash open the shells of animals they want to eat. A small group of dolphins in one bay in Australia use sponges to protect their mouths when they forage, like you might wear a glove, which they use to dig around on the seafloor for bottom-dwelling fish. In Indonesia, veined octopus hide inside discarded coconut shells when predators are near.

Making a tool, however, takes a lot more brain power and only a few animals are able to do it. New Caledonian crows create their own tools out of twigs, wood and whatever other things they can find, putting the tools together using their beak and feet. Researchers have found that they can assemble long thin tools from lots of small parts. With these, they fish for grubs, waiting until it latches on for them to pull the tool back. Or they just spear them.

The only other animals that can create tools are primates. That includes us! Our thumbs are very different from most other animals'. We can touch our thumb to our first finger for a start, which most animals cannot do. This is called the "opposable thumb" and scientists think this developed so that our primate ancestors could climb about in the trees and grip on to branches. This thumb then became useful for when these primates were on land as it meant they could make basic tools.

Chimpanzees are well-known tool makers – making spearing tools out of twigs to fish for termites and forming sponges out of mashed-up leaves that they drink from. But by this point, chimpanzees had had quite a lot of airtime. Gorillas, on the other hand, had rarely been filmed. So, David set out to try to find some.

EASTERN GORILLA

Gorilla beringei (gore-ill-ah bear-in-gee-aye)

There are two species of gorilla, western and eastern, each of which has two sub-species. The two sub-species of eastern gorilla are the lowland group that live in the Congo, and the mountain gorillas that David and his team went to see.

Eastern Gorilla

Gorillas are very large, strong apes with black skin and hair. Males have an extra silver patch on their back that looks a little like a saddle.

Their arms are fifteen to twenty per cent longer than their back legs as they mostly walk on all fours. They have wide nostrils and a heavy brow – they often look a bit like they're thinking deeply about something complicated.

Despite how fearsome they might look, gorillas are vegetarians, and most of their time is spent foraging and sleeping. As well as eating shoots, roots and flowers, they very occasionally eat their own poo! We think they do this to absorb all the nutrients they can from the hard-to-break-down seeds and roughage they eat.

They are one of the calmest species of ape, and are very good at problem solving. As well as good-mannered burping, gorillas have a number of other barks and grunts they make, depending on the situation.

Chest beating is done when the group might

feel threatened. This is quite literally beating their chest to make a deep noise. Both males and females do it, but it's louder in males because they have huge air sacs in their throat and chest to resonate the sound.

Gorillas are at risk due to habitat destruction, catching human diseases, and hunting, and the IUCN lists the mountain gorilla as an endangered species. We think there are about 1,000 left in the wild.

SUB-SPECIES

Species are split into sub-species when they live in completely different places and so may have different diets and habits. They usually get an extra species name in their Latin name, so that you can tell them apart. The two sub-species of eastern gorilla are completely separated by their habitats (mountains and lowland), and so they eat different food and also might have developed different behaviour related to their habitat. They haven't changed enough genetically to be called separate species, but that could happen over time as their populations continue to live separately.

Dr Dian Fossey had been studying gorillas who lived in the Virunga Mountains (a row of extinct volcanoes) in Rwanda; the troop were familiar enough with humans that people could get close enough to film them. Dian was very protective of the gorillas but agreed to let David and his team come and film. One of the gorillas, named Digit, had recently been killed by hunters, and she hoped the programme might mean better protection. And so, in 1978, David, director John Sparks, Dickie Bird the sound man and Martin Saunders the cameraman set off together to create what would turn out to be one of the most iconic moments of natural history television ever shown.

DR DIAN FOSSEY

- Dian Fossey was a prominent researcher and primatologist, which is a person who studies primates such as apes, monkeys and humans.

- Her most notable work was a study that focused on gorillas in the mountain forests of Rwanda, where she studied groups of gorillas closely, in an attempt to learn about their behaviour.

- She later published her findings in a book called *Gorillas in the Mist* (1983).

Dr Dian Fossey

When they arrived in Rwanda, Dian was sick with malaria so instructed an assistant called Ian to guide them to two of the gorilla groups they studied. Ian explained that he would have to introduce David and his team to the gorillas, in the hope that they would allow them to get close. To do this, they would have to behave just like a gorilla, and that meant burping.

Gorillas live in very thick vegetation and in order to keep track of each other, they burp as they move around – scientists call this belch vocalisations, or BVs for short. It's very good manners for visitors to do the same. Not least because surprising a gorilla could be dangerous!

They were also told to keep their voices low and not to stare, keeping their heads low to show they were no threat to the gorillas. This is something we do too – think about when people bow to each other to show respect.

David tried to remember all this as they tracked the group through the thick plants on the mountainside. Now if you ever meet a gorilla, you know exactly what to do too!

"TRACKING GORILLAS IN SUCH COUNTRY WAS HARDLY MORE DIFFICULT THAN TRACKING A STEAMROLLER. THEY LEAVE A BROAD PATH OF FLATTENED VEGETATION IN THEIR WAKE."

It wasn't long before they found the gorillas. Ian made sure they were visible from a long way away so that the gorillas could see them approaching. As they got closer, Ian signalled that it was time for the team to start burping! A guard gorilla high up in the tree watched as David approached slowly, then returned to eating. That was a sign that they were allowed to visit. They stayed for a few moments, before the gorillas moved on. The second day they returned to the same troop of gorillas with their cameras, which the gorillas didn't seem to mind either.

The team visited them over a few days. David was overcome with emotion when he came face to face with a pair of young gorillas, Titus and

Kweli, who were playing. He decided this wasn't the time to talk about tool use or opposable thumbs. He ignored the script he had researched and written especially for this episode. Instead, he turned to the camera and talked about how like humans they were.

"THERE IS MORE MEANING AND MUTUAL UNDERSTANDING IN EXCHANGING A GLANCE WITH A GORILLA THAN ANY OTHER ANIMAL I KNOW."

Their last day with the gorillas meant even closer contact. A female gorilla called Puck sat alone eating wild celery and he stretched out beside her, turning back to face the camera. Before he could begin talking, she reached out and rested her hand on his head and began to play with his hair. She pulled his lip to look inside his mouth, while a young gorilla called Pablo climbed on top of him and others tried to steal his shoes. After the gorillas left, David realized Martin had only filmed a little bit as they were almost out of film! They were also wary about showing such playful footage of gorillas, in case people back home assumed they were tame. David couldn't believe the experience he'd just had.

When they arrived back in the UK, David and some of Dian's previous students set up a fund for the gorillas so that people who watched the show could donate money for their protection and research. While ecotourism is a big way of funding gorilla conservation, we are now no longer allowed to get quite so close to gorillas.

They share ninety-eight per cent of our genes, so are very similar to us, but this means they can easily catch our illnesses. It is a privilege to be able to visit the gorillas, but it's important we keep them safe.

The first episode of *Life on Earth* was shown in January 1979, and things started quietly, but by the last episode, 14 million people were tuning in. It was nominated for and won a number of awards and was shown in a hundred countries. It was an enormous success, showing that people really did want to learn more about the natural world.

THE LIVING PLANET

After the success of *Life on Earth*, David decided he wanted to look at the different environments across the world. Each episode would explore a type of biome and look at the clever ways living things have adapted, through natural selection, to live there. This series would be called *The Living Planet* and was first shown on the BBC in 1984.

A biome is a type of place with particular characteristics. Some people say the five major biome types are: desert, aquatic, forest, grassland and tundra. However, you could equally divide them up into aquatic (water-based) and terrestrial (on-land) habitats. Some people also include mountains, islands and wetlands, and they might split "aquatic" into freshwater and marine. There's not really one right explanation! Sometimes science doesn't have clear rules, even though it might look like it does.

BIOME

You might think of a biome as a very big ecosystem or lots of habitats. A habitat is the environment that an animal or plant lives in. Your home, and the town you live in, is your habitat. Habitats are made up by a number of factors, including the weather today and its pattern over the year, how much water is nearby and what kind of water there is (if there is any), how warm or cold it is, what food is available and how much shelter there is.

For some species, other factors are important in their habitats – for plants it will matter how much light there is or how damp the soil might be. As we learned in the sections about evolution and natural selection, species adapt to the habitat they live in over time.

A habitat doesn't have to be a large geographical area. If you're a very small creature, your entire habitat might be a rock or a log or, if you are a parasite or a tiny single-celled organism, even the insides of another creature's body!

ECOSYSTEM

When we want to think about the physical features of a habitat and the animals and plants living in and interacting with it, we call this an ecosystem. You might hear people talking about how nature is in balance. Usually what they are talking about are ecosystems, and how everything works together because of how animals and plants have adapted to the habitat alongside each other.

A simple way of thinking about ecosystems is to imagine a place that contains rabbits, foxes and greenery. Rabbits eat the grass and plants and foxes eat the rabbits. When the foxes and the rabbits die, nutrients from the animals' bodies are released into the soil, which the plants use to grow. You might think of it as a big circle, in which "matter" (the stuff we're made of) is recycled by all the different living things.

You might be wondering how all these different habitats and biomes formed. Our planet is made up of lots of layers of rock and metal. We can group these into four big layers, which have lots of smaller layers within them.

Inner core: this is a super-hot core that sits right in the middle; it is thought to be the same temperature as the sun.

Outer core: this sits around the inner core and is liquid rock – sometimes we call this molten rock or magma.

Mantle: this is the next layer and is thick solid rock in several layers where the rocks get hotter and harder the closer to the core they get. This the biggest layer!

Crust: this is the top layer of the mantle that has cooled and gone hard – it's the land we live on.

These layers are always moving. The top layer of our planet is split up into tectonic plates that look like big puzzles pieces, which are chunks of the crust and outer mantle together. There are seven large ones and dozens of smaller ones. When plates move and bump into each other, we get earthquakes. In these gaps or where the crust is thin, we often find volcanoes.

Think of a volcano as a huge chimney from the crust all the way down to the outer core. They occasionally erupt, which means magma explodes from the top of them. This happens because the magma pushes up this chimney, building pressure as it goes, causing the gases in there to expand and water to heat up so much that it becomes steam. When the pressure is too much, the volcano erupts, and the magma, which we then call lava, streams out. When we think of volcanoes, you might think of a cone or mountain shape, but they come in lots of different shapes and sizes. There are volcanoes on every continent, on the seafloor and under the ice caps.

When the lava spills out and cools, it forms

hard rock, and so can create whole new bits of land or landforms. Over many billions of years, volcanoes created more than eighty per cent of our planet's surface!

ACTIVE VOLCANOES

We've come across animals living in extinct volcanoes so far, but did you know that some animals live inside active volcanoes?

In the ocean around the Solomon Islands near Papua New Guinea, researchers travelled out to film at an underwater volcano called Kavachi, dropping the camera into a crater over 44 metres below sea level. On the footage, they saw silky sharks, stingrays and scalloped hammerhead sharks swimming about inside the volcano!

We still don't know if they always live there but given how hot and acidic the water would be, scientists were very surprised to see them.

Scientists even plan on electronically tagging sharks in the area to learn more about their visits to the volcano.

active volcano

David was very keen to include a volcano in the first episode of *The Living Planet*, but it would be even better if he could find one that was erupting. Volcanoes don't erupt all the time, and plenty are extinct. Luckily, some scientists in Iceland promised David that they would keep an eye on their active volcanoes and let him know in case one erupted so they could film. One afternoon, when he was sat in a very boring meeting, a note arrived to say one of the Icelandic volcanoes was about to erupt and he had to leave right away! It was a real race against time. What if they arrived and it had stopped erupting? This was a rare chance to film something truly spectacular.

Jane raced him to the airport, where he met with mountaineer and director Ned Kelly and they boarded the next flight to Reykjavik. After several flights, they arrived in the town near the volcano at three in the morning, and piled on to snowmobiles, racing through the bitterly cold weather to get there in time. In the distance, they began to see a spray of bright scarlet shooting up into the sky, surrounded by thick black clouds. They hopped off the snowmobiles and walked, the howling wind blowing ash into their faces. As they grew closer, fine ash began to fall around them and, despite the icy wind, the heat from the volcano burnt at their skin. They found a spot that was as close as they could get without melting their equipment, or themselves.

"THIS FANTASTIC FOUNTAIN OF FIRE RISING 200 FEET OR SO INTO THE AIR BEHIND ME IS MOLTEN ROCK. FINE ASH IS FALLING ALL AROUND. THERE ARE GUSTS OF CHOKING POISONOUS GAS, AND IT'S SO HOT THAT THIS IS JUST ABOUT AS CLOSE AS I CAN GET TO IT."

It took them thirty hours to get there, film as much footage as they could and set off again for home. It was a whirlwind adventure to get as close to the creation of new land as possible.

One of the most ground-breaking things about *The Living Planet* was the final episode, in which David looked at the many ways humans have changed the world – how we have damaged the planet and altered entire habitats, just so we can grow crops or raise livestock or put up some skyscrapers or build a big road.

It might seem surprising to you that this was one of the first times that what we call "human impacts" on the environment was really shown on television.

There are several different types of human impact on the environment:

- burning fossil fuels
- pollution
- deforestation
- overfishing and unsustainable hunting and farming

FOSSIL FUELS

A fossil fuel is what we call natural gas, coal and crude oil. As the name might suggest, these are formed from the fossilised and buried remains of living things from millions of years ago.

When these living things break down, they release the carbon in their bodies, which is the key element of several types of fuel. There are a lot of problems with using fossil fuels:

1. Getting access to the fuel, which is deep down in the ground or under the sea, usually involves drilling, digging or fracking, which damages land.

2. In order to move the fuel around, pipelines, waste processing plants, roads and wells need to be built and maintained. It all adds up and divides up the landscape.

3. This all creates and leaves behind waste – including acid runoff from coal mining, rock and soil dumped in streams, and oil spills, which all pollute our water systems. These all include dangerous substances like radioactive materials and heavy metals. These can harm or kill the living things that rely on those water sources, and have even been found in some drinking water.

4. Processing and unearthing fossil fuels releases dangerous chemicals into the air, before you even burn them. Toxic particles in the air can get into people's lungs and cause serious health problems, like blood disorders and several types of cancer. So not only are we harming the environment, but these processes put the people working on them and those living and working nearby at risk.

There is an eco-friendly alternative to these fossil fuels that we call "green" energy types, or renewable resources. This means they are replaced naturally and fairly quickly, unlike fossil fuels that take millions of years to form.

PLASTIC POLLUTION

Plastics take a very long time to degrade and so any left in a forest, for example, would be there for hundreds of years, slowly breaking down into tiny bits of plastic. When plastic is left on a beach or thrown overboard, it gets moved around. Due to ocean currents, huge amounts wash up on islands or beaches after storms, where it might be dragged out to sea once again.

Great Pacific Garbage Patch

Sometimes the plastic bunches together in a big floating mess. The most famous of these is the Great Pacific Garbage Patch, which is a huge floating mass of plastic between Hawaii and California of 100,000 tonnes of plastic and is 1.6 million square kilometres in size. That's a hard amount to visualize, so imagine two Texases or three Frances, and that's how big that pile of plastic is! There are five offshore zones in the world's oceans where plastic gathers like this.

DEFORESTATION

Deforestation involves cutting or burning down trees. Trees are very important, not just because they provide homes and food for other living things, but because they convert carbon dioxide in our air to oxygen. When we breathe air, our lungs take in the oxygen and pass it around our body in our bloodstream to all our organs. What we breathe out is carbon dioxide, a by-product of these processes in our body. So you can see that animals that breathe air, including us, and trees (and all plants) have a very special relationship that depends on each other.

Areas of forest are usually cleared to build things or grow crops or to farm animals on them. When this happens, the forest is broken up into fragments, separated by gaps where humans use the land. This interrupts the habitat ranges of lots of animals. Palm-oil farming in Indonesia has led to intense habitat fragmentation of the forest, which dramatically affects orangutans and their large roaming ranges. Less space to roam, less food to eat – the animals' entire existence is threatened, even before this brings them into contact with poachers.

OVERFISHING

A huge impact humans have had on the seas is by overfishing. When we fish too much, we take away more animals from a population than are born in the same time period. This means that their overall population number goes down.

Fishers also are more likely to target big fish as that's more meat for us to eat. However, fish tend to get bigger as they grow older and produce more eggs and sperm, so when we take the biggest ones, we are also removing the ones that make the most babies. This also massively affects how many will be born and again means that overall population might go down.

When we talk about fish, we use the term "stock" or "fishery" to talk about a population of a species in a certain area. For the types of fish we eat, ninety per cent of the fish stocks or populations are either fished to their limit or are overfished. There is also a lot of illegal and unregulated fishing that happens around the world, and fishing with destructive methods like dynamite blasting or poisoning.

Managing and protecting our fish stocks is a very difficult thing to do, but it's essential. If we overfish, we can completely throw off ecosystems. A very famous example that David talks about in the last episode of *The Living Planet* is the Peruvian anchovy.

If you think back to the example of a simple

ecosystem (on page 143), it contained a few animals and plants, and the whole system fed into each other. Here, the ecosystem includes anchovies, Guanay cormorants (a type of sea bird) and green algae. The Guanay cormorant exclusively eats anchovies, and its poo has very rich nutrients that accumulate on the rocks, and was once collected and sold as fertilizer.

Its poo would also fall into the sea where it fertilized green algae, which the anchovies fed on. This created a very simple system of: green algae–anchovy–cormorant and back again. The anchovies also fed lots of big sea fish, like tuna.

When this type of fertilizer was less in fashion, the local people turned to the anchovies, catching millions of tonnes of them every year. The little nutrient-rich oily fish wasn't in demand for people to eat, but used to feed cattle, pigs and chickens. The fishing was so intense that the anchovies were almost wiped out, and so was the Guanay cormorant population. Few anchovies meant no food for the cormorants, and no guano meant no fertilizer for the algae which meant no food for the anchovies. No anchovies also meant no more large fish. On the islands David visits, there are now one-fiftieth of the population that used to live there. We call this complete wipeout of an ecosystem at all levels a "trophic cascade".

"THROUGH THAT ONE RASH ACT OF OVERFISHING THIRTY YEARS AGO, PERU HAS LOST ANCHOVIES, CORMORANTS, GUANO AND SEA FISH. IT'S A MAJOR BLOW TO THE NATION'S ECONOMY."

This series started out looking at the ways animals can adapt to their own habitats, and ended with a stark warning that we need to look after our planet – and all the things that inhabit it – much better.

THE TRIALS OF LIFE

In between *Life on Earth* and *The Living Planet* David found himself doing all sorts of odd jobs for the BBC. One day, he even recorded the Queen's speech from inside the stables in Buckingham Palace, and had to ask her politely to do a second take because one of the horses was chewing and it looked like he was copying her!

He'd looked at evolution and different habitats, so what to explore next? It seemed the next big thing to look at would be behaviour. Zoology as a science had changed a lot since he was at Cambridge, when it was all laboratories and examining animals' bodies after they had died. He'd found it all a bit stuffy. A whole new branch of science had ventured out into nature to look at the ways animals interacted with each other and the world around them.

David decided the best place to start would be birth – the very first trial any creature faces.

Like with *The Living Planet*, he knew he needed an impressive first shot, but what was the erupting volcano equivalent in animals? He figured another impressive mass spawning would be just right. They'd been lucky with the horseshoe crabs all those years ago. What could they find that was similar? It turned out this time to be an actual crab, rather than an isopod that kind of looked like one.

The red crab migration is one of the most impressive spectacles of the natural world. Christmas Island is a small Australian island in the Indian Ocean, south of Indonesia. As soon as the first rainfall of the wet season hits the island, the little bright red crabs start appearing, usually around October or November, all determined by the phase of the moon. The moon and our ocean tides are linked, and the crabs always spawn before dawn as the high tide goes out when the last quarter of the moon can be seen in the sky. All the crabs on the island march towards the ocean to mate, making the beaches appear totally red as they release billions of fertilized eggs into the sea.

It is a very delicate matter of timing, and David knew this. He was used to racing across the world to get the perfect shot, but what he didn't expect was an airline strike on the day he arrived in mainland Australia. The crew had mere hours to get to the island in order to find the right filming locations and catch this amazing experience on camera. Luckily, the director, Alastair Fothergill, managed to convince an army cargo plane to give them a lift – it was very, very cold and noisy, but they made it.

Looking around the island, they could see no crabs at all. Had they missed it? They asked the islanders, who said yes, there were crabs around but they were very good at hiding. And, luckily, they'd not missed the spawning. There was still time.

On the evening that was predicted for the crabs to appear, David and his team waited on a deserted beach of black volcanic rock. There was not a crab to be seen. They waited and waited. And suddenly, in the dark, their torches caught the shiny red back of a crab.

Hundreds appeared over the next few minutes,

and then thousands. During the spawning, there were one hundred crabs per square metre of beach or rock. The clear sea water began to look brownish-black with all the eggs released into it.

As David spoke to the camera about the red crabs, several began crawling up his trousers. Ever the professional, he soldiered on and hoped they wouldn't pinch his bottom.

CHRISTMAS ISLAND RED CRAB

Gecarcoidea natalis (gee-car-coy-dia nat-arl-is)

These bright red little crabs are omnivorous scavengers that will eat pretty much whatever they can find – fruit, plants, human rubbish, other dead crabs and, their favourite, giant African land snails.

Despite spending their larval stage in the sea, the Christmas Island red crab is actually a land crab. They live in the forests of Christmas Island in burrows. They cannot swim, so depositing their eggs on the shore is dangerous business! In the early 1990s, scientists estimated how many adult crabs might live there and suggested there were 43.7 million adult crabs on the island. The same scientists found that generally the crabs went to the beaches on the northwest shore to spawn, no matter how far away from it they were, walking hundreds and hundreds of metres in a day to get there.

The larvae grow in the sea for several weeks, each one looking a bit like a tiny prawn, before eventually growing enough to look like a little crab, five millimetres across. So many eggs and larvae are released because most don't make it back to land, and instead are eaten by lots of fish, including massive whale sharks.

The crabs have no natural predators, but

an accidental introduction of an invasive ant species killed between 10 and 15 million crabs, and so Christmas Island set up a panel of people to monitor and control the ant population, in order to protect the crabs and the ecosystem as a whole.

To further protect the red crabs, Christmas Island closes many of its roads during the spawning season and has built big bridges over main roads so that the crabs can cross safely. Lots of people come to visit the national park every year to see the crab migration.

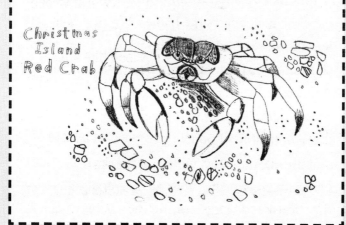

Christmas Island Red Crab

Animals have evolved lots of clever ways to mate and give birth. We'll learn a bit more about how animals choose mates in a later chapter. So far we've looked at asexual reproduction, temperature-dependent sex determination, and mass spawning, but let's take a moment to talk about another unusual way of raising babies.

In most animals it is the females that get pregnant or lay eggs. Mammals like us grow young animals in their wombs, reptiles and birds incubate their eggs by keeping them warm until they hatch, and amphibians and fish lay their eggs in little clusters underwater that they protect until they hatch.

Pipefish decided to mix things up a little and have the males carry the babies. When a male and female get ready to mate, they do a very intricate courtship display of wriggling and shaking – think of it like a really good dance. The female passes her eggs over to the male, where he raises them in his brood pouch.

The males of the group of fish that includes pipefish, seahorses and seadragons all carry the fertilized eggs until the babies hatch.

The group's name is Sygnathidae, which is a bit of a mouthful. They all have slightly different ways of doing it. Seahorses have full pockets sort of like a female kangaroo does, while seadragons just stick them on to their tails. Pipefish do a mix of both. Sometimes when the eggs are stuck to them, flaps of skin grow around the eggs in order to protect them. The brood pouches (which is what we call all of them, even the sticky surfaces) can be on their tummies or their tail.

The males carry these eggs until the tiny pipefish (or seahorses or seadragons) hatch out and swim away from their father.

SEX AND GENDER

In this book you'll have seen us talk about male and female animals. This refers to their sex and ultimately what reproductive organs and chromosomes they have.

"Sex" determines how you reproduce and what levels of hormones your body uses when you go through puberty. It's not always as simple as "male or female", as we know that many animals and people can have a mix of both organs and chromosomes – this is called being intersex.

On the other hand, when we talk about if someone is a boy, a girl or non-binary we are talking about their gender, not their sex. Some people describe gender as what you feel or know you are – it's about how you see yourself.

Sometimes people are born with a gender identity that doesn't align with their sex, and so may experience serious distress about their outside appearance not matching up to how they feel on the inside – we call this gender dysphoria. These people may transition, perhaps by changing their name or pronouns, or taking medication so they go through the opposite-sex puberty.

We don't know if animals have any concept

of gender so we refer to them as male or female when discussing their sex – but it's important to remember that sex and gender aren't the same thing.

Be respectful and kind when people tell you the name and pronoun they'd like you to use for them, even if it's a little different from what you expected.

TEAMWORK MAKES
THE DREAM WORK

Teamwork has always been key to our species' success. The way humans have been able to communicate and cooperate has helped us thrive in environments all over the planet (even if we're often not very good at doing either).

David wanted to show teamwork at its best, its quickest and its smartest. He would have to go hunting. He had heard of a regularly studied group of chimpanzees who had been observed working together to hunt monkeys.

This was very different from the quite calm group of chimpanzees that the scientist Dr Jane Goodall studied in Tanzania. No, Professor Christophe Boesch's Ivory Coast troupe were whip-smart, and David was hopeful that they would let his team come and see them and hopefully film a hunt.

DR JANE GOODALL

Dr Jane Goodall

- Jane Goodall is a renowned English primatologist and anthropologist.
- She is most recognized for her work on wild chimpanzees, in which she studied social and family interactions for sixty years.

- Her research challenged two common beliefs: that only humans could construct and use tools, and that chimpanzees were vegetarians.
- Jane Goodall continues to advocate for the protection of chimpanzees and their habitats.
- She and David have worked closely together on several conservation and environmental campaigns.
- Jane has a number of titles and achievements:

  – in 2002, she was named a UN Messenger of Peace

  – she founded the Jane Goodall Institute in 1977, a global wildlife and environment conservation organisation

  – she has been on the board of the Nonhuman Rights Project since it was originally founded in 1996

  – she is an honorary member of the World

Future Council
– she was made a Dame of the British Empire in 2004 (this is the equivalent of receiving a knighthood).

Jane Goodall and David Attenborough

Christophe was a very brusque Swiss man who had been following this group of chimpanzees for ten years. It took a long time but they were now accustomed to the strange, pale man who ran around after them, and so he was very strict that David's team should dress in similar clothes to his and behave as he did. That meant no talking, and lots of running after the chimpanzees when needed, so that they could track them.

Mike Richards, the cameraman, and Trevor Gosling, who worked on sound, were young and fit, so this would be easy for them. Christophe asked, quite firmly, if David – who was now in his mid-sixties – could keep up with all the running. David assured him that he could.

Studying chimpanzees is quite an intensive job. Christophe would follow the chimpanzees around all day, noting down what they were doing and when, in a specific way that allowed him to build up a lot of information about chimpanzees over time. It's ideal to not have a break in any of this data – no missed days, no distractions – because it creates a better record and timeline of the group being studied.

There are a few ways that behavioural biologists do this: they might scan the whole group and note down what every member is doing at particular time intervals, or they might focus on a few individuals and follow their habits over a certain period of time. This way, scientists can understand how individual animals behave and what they do with their time across the day but also how they behave in a group.

Christophe would follow the group every day until they started making their nests for the night, so that he knew where to find them the next day. This sounds quite reasonable, but if your chimpanzees are nesting far away from where you live, you have to get up extremely early so they don't leave before you arrive.

That meant on the first day David and the team went out with him they had to get up at 4 a.m. and run through the rainforest. After a few hours of tripping and stumbling in the dark, they found the chimpanzee group. They collapsed to the floor, happy to catch their breath, only for all sixty chimpanzees to get up and set off for their morning adventure. Typical!

They followed them in much the same way for the next few days, racing after them but keeping a quiet distance and filming what they could. Five days in and they hadn't seen them hunt once, though they had watched them annoy an ant colony by scooping larvae out from their nest and dashing off with it. Would they see them chase the monkeys? And if they saw it, would they even be able to film it?

On the sixth day, as they followed the chimpanzees, David heard some soft grunting noises. It was a group of black-and-white colobus monkeys feeding, and the chimpanzees had spotted them. The females and young chimpanzees stopped, while a group of young males gathered together on the forest floor watching the canopy above them, tracking the monkeys. Mike filmed constantly, following each of the chimpanzees while David hurriedly explained into the microphone what was happening. All this, of course, was done while chasing the chimpanzees.

Two younger males, the blockers, climbed up trees so they were either side of the colobus monkeys, while an older male ran off into the brush, disappearing from sight. Suddenly, two other young males rushed up the trees on the attack, driving the monkeys forward.

The colobus monkeys began to move in one direction, but the blockers appeared, screeching loudly! The terrified monkeys turned and ran a different way ... straight towards the hidden older male. The trap was closed. He caught one, and suddenly the hunt was over. Around them, the whole troupe let out a terrifying chorus of excited screams as the meal was divided between the group.

What David had seen and managed to film was not just chimpanzees working together as a team, but working in clear roles. Think of it like a football match – everyone's position is important but they all have different roles to play. Defenders stop the opposite team from getting too close to the goal, while forwards push everyone forward, so that strikers can try to score. Everyone has their own role and by working together you can be successful.

This was the final scene of the fourth episode

of *The Trials of Life*, in which David, exhausted and soaked with sweat, turned to the camera to address the eerie scene.

"THESE BLOODSTAINED FACES MAY WELL HORRIFY US, BUT WE MIGHT ALSO SEE IN THEM THE FACE OF OUR LONG-DISTANT HUNTING ANCESTORS. AND IF WE ARE APPALLED BY THAT MOB VIOLENCE AND BLOODLUST,

WE MIGHT ALSO SEE
IN THAT, PERHAPS, THE
ORIGINS OF TEAMWORK
THAT HAVE, IN THE END,
BROUGHT HUMAN BEINGS
MANY OF THEIR GREATEST
TRIUMPHS."

THE ART OF COMMUNICATION

All these behaviours rely on one crucial thing – communication. If you can't communicate that you're hungry or scared, how will other animals be able to tell what you need? While animals can't 'talk' in the same way we do with specific words for things and concepts, there are lots of ways that animals communicate through colour, sound, movement and even dance.

David's episode on communication, "Talking to Strangers", showcases some of the best and brightest communication methods between animals.

One of the most interesting and complex vocal communication systems comes from vervet monkeys in Kenya. Vervet monkeys spend a lot of their time in trees but come down to the ground to feed, which puts them at risk from predators.

Scientists studying the vervet monkeys found that they would sound an alarm call if a predator was nearby, but the rest of the group would respond differently – sometimes they would run up a tree or look a particular way. These calls all sounded slightly different too, but what was happening?

Vervet monkeys

The scientists recorded their calls and noted down which predators were nearby, and what the monkeys did after the call. They found three different alarm calls and responses:

- **Alarm call one:** leopards are nearby – all the vervet monkeys run up into the trees away from the leopard.

- **Alarm call two:** eagles are overhead – all the monkeys look up to watch out for the eagles and run into thick brush or the trees so that the birds cannot easily get to them.

- **Alarm call three:** there's a snake! All the monkeys look down and in the direction of where the alarm caller is looking (this is called attenuation, like when someone is looking at something you can't see, and you stop to see what it could be).

Another extremely complicated vocal system belongs to the dolphin. Dolphins are very social animals who live in groups called pods.

They make two kinds of noises that you can hear both underwater and when they are at the surface: clicks and whistles. While their clicks are used to see what's near them by bouncing sound waves off it (we call this echolocation), their whistles make up a complicated language. It's thought that each dolphin has its own whistle name and that young dolphins inherit name-whistles that sound a little like their mothers', sort of like surnames in humans.

When they find food, bottlenose dolphins whistle more frequently; it's thought to attract more dolphins to help round up the school of fish. Dolphins do make other sounds too, when they're hurt or angry or mating – buzzing clicks, yelps or even just making their calls very, very loud. We know that their posture is also important in communicating, though we're still trying to understand why, so a wag of their head or bending their tail a certain way may completely change the meaning of their "words". They also use physical touch a lot, perhaps by nuzzling into another dolphin or whacking them with their tail.

There's been a lot of research into whether

dolphin-speak is a true language like ours – whether they can tell stories or talk about things that aren't around them in the moment. There was even a study funded by NASA in the 1960s to see if dolphins could learn English, in which a woman called Margaret Howe Lovatt lived in a submerged house with a dolphin called Peter. There is still so much to learn about the way they speak and how they combine sounds and physical gestures, but David summed it up well after swimming with a pod of dolphins.

"THE RESULT IS AN AMAZINGLY COMPLEX WEB OF COMMUNICATION UNEXCELLED BY ANY OTHER ANIMAL, EXCEPT OURSELVES. BUT HOW MARVELLOUS IT WOULD BE IF WE COULD BECOME PART OF THAT."

To communicate with sound you don't have to use your voice. In one scene, David wanders out into scrubland and attaches a clever bit of technology called a geophone to the ground near some molehills. The one he used transformed any vibrations in the ground into sounds that we humans can hear. Once he had plugged in, David knocked on the ground, like you might knock on someone's door. A few moments later, something underground returned a distinct thudding knock. It turned out David was communicating with a hairy mole rat.

These hairy mole rats are completely blind – why have sight when you live in total darkness? – and also have quite bad hearing. The thuds they create vibrate along their tunnels and are felt through their bodies which they press up against the walls.

Hairy mole rats are very anti-social, and these thuds alert other mole rats to where they are, so they can avoid each other. It's a bit like yelling "DON'T TALK TO ME" in a busy playground to make sure no one comes up to bother you. But how do they make these noises? Well, by banging their head against the tunnel ceiling, of course. I'm sure you agree that this would be a very challenging communication method for people that would result in a lot of sore heads!

Communication methods can make a lot of sense for one animal depending on their bodies and how they live and interact with others, but can seem very silly when we humans think about doing it.

Communication also doesn't have to happen between two animals of the same species. It might surprise you to learn that some animals communicate with their predators.

Gazelles will perform acrobatic jumps as they run to signal to whatever animal is hunting them that, actually, I'm really, really fit, so fit that you probably can't catch me and are just going to tire yourself out, so you may as well give up! It's surprisingly effective and sensible when you consider that predators don't want to exhaust themselves just for one meal when they're already hungry.

Animals don't just show predators how fit they are in order to not get eaten. They can also do the opposite and trick their enemy into thinking they are much weaker. Ringed plover birds lay their eggs on open shingle beaches. The eggs are easily camouflaged but the birds themselves are much less so, and are easy for predators to spot. To distract the predators from looking for the eggs, the plovers run off, dragging one of their wings behind them and making a noise like a sad cry. This makes predators think they are hurt and easy prey that will require very little energy for them to catch. Once the plover has led the predator far enough away from the nest, they will simply fly off, leaving a confused predator behind.

That's right, animals can lie! Your parents and teachers have probably told you that lying isn't very good, and that's true – but these animals are lying as a matter of survival, so we'll let them off.

BIRDS OF PARADISE (FINALLY!)

"OK, I WAS A BIOLOGIST ONCE, BUT I'M A HOPELESS BIRDER. IF I GO OUT WITH A BIRDER, I KEEP MY MOUTH SHUT. I JUST NOD."

David knew that his next specific animal group series had to be about birds. By this point, he'd explored the world of Antarctica in his short series *Life in the Freezer* and had dived into the world of plants. While he has never been the sort of person who (in his own words!) can "identify a bird from a glimpse or a silhouette", he had always sought out the most complex of bird behaviours for his programmes. He knew that the show would be very popular, as British people love to go birdwatching.

And where better to start than his favourite group of birds, the birds of paradise. On several attempts he had tried to film birds of paradise in all their regal splendour early on in his career but had not been particularly lucky. *Zoo Quest* adventures had brought him close but not close enough on two occasions.

The Indonesian government didn't want him to travel to the island where the birds of paradise were as they thought he was a spy, and their trip to New Guinea in 1957 specifically for the birds of paradise yielded only a handful of shots of a single Count Raggi's bird in black and white. The camera they'd used needed to be wound up and was very loud – and they still couldn't record sound and film at the same time. David had only managed to record a very short clip of the bird's calls, which he had to loop to show along with the footage, which was much longer than the bird's few waa-waa calls. After watching it, his old zoology professor wrote congratulating him and remarking how strange the call was, as it had two identical component parts and had consistent spacing despite what was happening on screen. He suggested David write a scientific paper about his findings. David had to sheepishly write to him and explain he'd looped the singing!

But now it was the mid-nineties and he was in his seventies. David knew this was probably going to be his last chance, and so off to New Guinea they went. This time round they were much luckier.

On one of the days they went out to film, David was hoisted into the trees on a rope-pulley system to bring him close to an area where the greater bird-of-paradise tended to perform. These pigeon-sized birds have bright green bibs and red-brown bodies and wings, with striking orange fluffy feathers that stand up from their back, which they move about in display to attract a female.

David found himself close to a group of a dozen males. They seemed unbothered by his presence, but as soon as a female appeared in the tree among them, they all began to crow and dance. They flipped their heads down, waggling their bright orange feathers in the air, shimmying along their branches. The female appeared to pick a particularly nice-looking male and hopped down to his perch. David was a little taken aback to see the male turn around and peck her. Yet, she didn't move. He pecked her again and again, and still she stayed. He even flicked her with his wings!

As David lowered himself down from the canopy, he asked his cameraman, Mike, if he'd managed to film any closer shots. Mike said of course, because it turned out all the females picked the same handsome male, so he always knew which bird to focus the camera on from his filming platform. One slightly odd mating dance down, many more to go.

The thrill wasn't lost on David, finally able to see and film birds that had enchanted him since he was a boy. On one occasion when he witnessed the complex mating dance of a Wilson's bird-of-paradise, his sound recordist,

a man named Dickie Bird, remarked that he could
hear David's heart beating over his microphone.

BIRDS OF PARADISE

The birds of paradise are around forty-five
species of small forest birds found in New
Guinea and its surrounding islands, all with
striking and unique feathers. They range
from tiny birds all the way to ones roughly
the size of a crow. Their colours vary from
bright burnished oranges to luminous
yellows and greens and blues, and hints of
deepest black.

They also have a wide range of feather
shapes and styles – long ribbon-like tail
feathers, shiny feather bibs on their chests,
ornate crest feathers on the tops of their
heads, and one even has tail feathers that
look like a bundle of wires!

These fancy feathers signify that the males are healthy and thus would be very good for the females to mate with, as her offspring would have then inherited his good genes. (It's all about the genes!)

All these birds have a particular style of attracting mates. Males will display their plumage for females to come and admire. All this standing around and looking attractive may seem quite lazy but it's actually a mating strategy called "lekking" – deer also do this, with females choosing the males with the best antlers to mate with.

The male birds-of-paradise use a mixture of colour, dancing, singing and even changing the shape of their bodies with displays of their wings to attract females.

Some species lift their ruff feathers so that they form a complete circle around their heads.

The superb bird-of-paradise does this and adds in a bright electric-blue strip that makes him look like he has a smiley face.

Overall, this group of birds look and act very differently despite being closely related.

Collectors in museums have historically been a little confused by birds of paradise, as the first specimens they received in the sixteenth century usually arrived deconstructed.

The people in New Guinea who collected them tended to chop off their legs and wings so that all the feathers on their bodies could be better admired, and information was somewhat lost in translation as these museums were convinced that the birds were both wingless and legless! This is why the Latin name for the greater bird-of-paradise, one of the first species brought to Europe, translates to "the legless bird from paradise".

Bird of Paradise
New Guinea

When you think of birds, chances are one of the first things you think of is the sounds they make – the chirping and tweeting. Like in the previous chapter, where we discovered different types of communication, birds have very complicated songs. If you get up early enough in the morning before dawn, you might hear all the birds in your area singing in what we call the "dawn chorus".

Birds can learn their songs in all kinds of ways, but they all have a special time period in which they learn them. If baby birds are raised without adults around, their songs will develop abnormally and not sound quite right, though they can learn some songs from recordings. Clearly, being around other birds and hearing their songs is essential for them to learn how to sing – just like how baby humans learn to talk!

For some birds, their songs are used to signify how healthy they are and attract a mate – an audio-only version of the birds of paradise's complicated mating dances. Their health and good genes might be shown by how long and complicated the single song is, or how many different songs they can learn, some of which they mimic from other birds. How big their collection of songs is often depends on the species.

One of the best examples of this is the Australian superb lyrebird. The lyrebird is about the size of a chicken with dark brown feathers on its body and a long feathered tail. Its tail is made up of many feathers, but its main feature is the two striking striped feathers, which were popular on hats in the 1800s. Despite their fancy plumage, it's their voices that are most interesting.

LYREBIRDS

Lyrebirds are mimics – they learn songs and sounds from their surroudings and incorporate them into their own original songs.

Male lyrebirds also have beautiful tails and they use their songs and their fancy tails in a complicated dance to attract females. Whereas recent studies have shown that female lyrebirds often use their songs to defend their territories and when protecting their young.

David was determined to film these birds in action, showing the wide range of their vocal talents. He wanted a shot of the lyrebird singing, with him also in the frame so that he could introduce the bird.

The dense forest the birds live in made it hard to film, but luckily, they came across a fallen log – David could hide at one end and his cameraman at the other, hoping they could encourage the lyrebird to jump on to the log in the middle and sing.

This sounds quite difficult but in his years of filming David had picked up a trick – the easiest way to get a bird to sing to you is to play back a recording of its song. They hid a speaker in the log and no sooner had it begun to play a lyrebird's song than a male rushed out of the dense brush and hopped up on to the log, hoping to chase off this (imaginary) interloping male from his territory. But he kept going, running past the log, and then realized the sound was behind him, so back he came, overshooting again. Feeling a little sorry for the confused bird, they managed to get a quick introduction from David in before they stopped using the recording.

To get the full sequence of the lyrebirds, the team used three birds: this wild male and two that lived in captivity, who were a little more used to having people around them. The most well-known lyrebird from these sequences was a bird called Chook from Adelaide Zoo, who had begun copying sounds of machinery around him. He was raised by zookeepers from a chick and so did a very good impression of one of them saying "Hello, Chook" as well as car alarms, camera shutters, and even the construction sounds of drills and saws that he had overheard when other zoo enclosures were being built. (Other captive lyrebirds have been shown to do very good impersonations of steam trains and even laser guns, pew pew pew!)

Another famous and spectacular way of attracting a mate is by building them a nest. Weaverbirds make complex nests out of folded twigs and mud, which they use to attract potential mates, sort of like saying, "Hey, look, I've built you a really nice house; want to come live in it?" One family of birds goes even a step further.

BOWERBIRDS

Bowerbirds are a family of birds whose males make complicated structures called "bowers", which they decorate with brightly coloured objects, fruit, leaves and sticks in order to attract a mate. These bowers aren't nests; they're just for show. Think of it more like building a beautiful gallery. They're usually built out of bent and arranged sticks.

There are about twenty species of bowerbirds, seventeen of which build these fancy structures which vary in size and shape.

In *The Life of Birds*, David filmed the Vogelkop bowerbird which makes covered bowers almost big enough for a person to crawl inside, whereas the satin bowerbirds, from his *Trials of Life* series, build U-shaped structures that barely reached his knee. The golden bowerbird lives in wet forest, where fungus grows on the twigs it uses to make its bower. This acts like a kind of glue, sticking the bower together and making it very stable.

Each bowerbird also has its own personal taste, just like we do. The first Vogelkop bowerbird they filmed decorated his bower with piles of bright pink flowers and shining beetle shell. Another used pomegranates, orange petals and dark little berries.

Meanwhile, the satin bowerbird clearly had a preference for the colour blue – blue flowers, blue shells and a blue parrot feather. The golden bowerbird's decoration of choice was tiny green and white flowers. They collect these treasured items over time, or might even steal from another unsuspecting male!

These mounds of treasures are displayed just so, for female birds that visit the bower with the intention of finding a mate.

Bowerbird and bower

All the same items tend to be grouped together in individual piles which he occasionally rearranges in a very particular way. David showed how important this was by cheekily moving the satin bowerbird's prize blue parrot feather, only for the male to grumpily hop down and put it back into position.

The females choose to have offspring with the male with the bower she likes best, so doing a good decorating job is very important!

Near the end of filming, David got an extremely sad phone call. His wife, Jane, had taken ill very suddenly. She had had a stroke, and was in a coma. He had to fly back from New Zealand, where he was filming at the time. He was able to get back to London in time to say goodbye with a hand squeeze and a few quiet words. Sadly, Jane died on the night before their forty-seventh wedding anniversary.

NO PHOTOS, PLEASE!

After *The Life of Birds*, David focused on a couple of different smaller projects, throwing himself into work in order to cope with the loss of Jane. One of his most well known was the narration for *Blue Planet* and *Planet Earth*, two series produced by Alastair Fothergill, with whom he had worked on *The Trials of Life*.

These are two programmes that are associated very much with David, as he wrote and performed the commentaries on them, just like in his *Life* series.

However, he was not involved with the production or filming and instead just wrote the words you hear spoken over the scenes of animals going about their business. In fact, David gets a little embarrassed when all the credit is given to him!

"YOU CHANGE THE PACE, YOU CHANGE THE TIMBRE, YOU CHANGE THE MOOD, AND THE COMMENTARY HAS ORGANIC FLOW ... IF THE LAST SENTENCE ENDED TEN SECONDS AGO RATHER THAN ONE MINUTE AGO, YOU START IN A DIFFERENT KIND OF WAY. I DON'T THINK OTHER PEOPLE DO THAT. IT'S A CRAFT, AND I QUITE ENJOY IT, ACTUALLY."

Filming technology had improved a lot since the early days of *Zoo Quest* and their enormous reels of film and wind-up cameras. The next few *Life* series and other programmes that David worked on all featured top-of-the-line technology that allowed things that had never been seen before to be filmed. Here are some of the clever techniques they used to show the best and brightest of nature!

TWO SHOTS

David realized cute furry mammals would make a popular series topic, but there was a problem. They'd covered a lot of the big mammals in their previous series. How could they prove that this was a brand-new series? The answer was to make sure David was in the picture too. They called this a "two shot".

Now, this sounds like it probably wouldn't be too difficult, right? They'd managed it with lots of animals before, and David was a professional. Well, *The Life of Mammals* would feature one creature that David was terribly afraid of, which he'd managed to avoid being around in most of his other programmes ... the rat. Yes, that's right. Rats. Of all the creatures in the world that he had seen, David was scared of rats. It sounds illogical, but that's phobias – you can be terribly afraid of something that you know isn't going to hurt you.

Anyway, after filming around grizzly bears and hedgehogs and all sorts of animals, they headed to the Karni Mata Temple, a Hindu temple in India where approximately 25,000 black rats live. David agreed that he would be in the shot with the rats, but soon realized, as it was a temple, that he would be doing it barefoot. His cameraman agreed that he would arrange for a tall stool to be brought in, so that David would be able to sit a little way above the rats and not be so nervous.

Of course, on the day that he arrived to film there, David caught his cameraman sneakily rubbing banana all over the legs of the stool, to entice the rats to climb up him! Realizing he had been caught, the cameraman simply shrugged and pointed out that the rats climbing up him would have made a better shot.

HOT OR COLD?

For his series on reptiles, *Life in Cold Blood*, David returned to the Galapagos to film some of the animals he'd filmed back in the *Zoo Quest* days, particularly the marine iguana. Like all reptiles, marine iguanas are ectotherms, like amphibians, fish and invertebrates. This means that they need to draw energy and heat directly from the sun, which they do by sunbathing. Mammals (like us) and birds can generate their own body heat, and so are endotherms.

These iguanas are very special because they exclusively eat algae and seaweed, meaning they dive into the water to get it. However, the sea around the Galapagos is very cold! So how do they manage it without getting too cold?

David and the team had a thermal camera with them. Thermal cameras detect heat to produce an image, showing how hot something is with different colours. What better to use it on than an ectothermic iguana?

In the morning, the iguanas would emerge from their shelters a deep blue, showing they were quite cold, ready to sunbathe on the rocks. Rather quickly, the colour would change, from purple-ish blue to red to orange to a golden yellow, showing they had warmed up a lot (to compare, a person's face usually shows up this colour on a thermal camera). Full of energy, they would dive for their meal of seaweed, turning bluer with every moment. After only a few minutes, they would return to the rocks totally blue, and start the process all over again.

TINY CAMERAS

For *The Life of Mammals*, David decided he'd like to film a platypus in its nest. Platypuses defy how we categorize animals because they are a mammal that lays eggs. He'd learned from years of filming that catching any egg hatching was challenging at the best of times, and platypuses live in burrows.

Thinking carefully, the team came up with a clever plan. They would locate a female platypus in her nest using radio tracking technology and would drill a small hole down to the burrow and film using an endoscope. An endoscope is a very long and thin tube-shaped camera that we use to look inside people's bodies.

They found a female, thanks to the help of some scientists, and traced her as she burrowed through the ground – a little like a mole – forcing her way through the earth in a tunnel. When she stopped moving, they realized she must have reached her nest. The cameraman nervously began to drill down, stopping just before the nest chamber. They slipped the endoscope down the hole and there was a curled-up platypus happily dozing. As they kept watching, they saw a movement and a shiny baby platypus.

baby Platypus

One impressive technique relied on very high definition camera technology: slow motion. Slow motion is a filming technique in which you capture many frames per second at a rate much faster than you would show it, which means that whatever you film appears to move at a slower rate than normal. Using this, they were able to film ants meeting each other, touching in greeting and occasionally swapping a little bubble of spit. This technique meant David and the team could capture the personalities and habits of tiny creatures, which we might not otherwise be able to see.

For *The Private Life of Plants*, the team used the reverse technique to film woodland plants. In time lapse photography, the rate of frames being filmed is much more spread out than the rate you would show it at. The camera operators would find an area of woodland, set up their camera, and leave it there over several weeks where it would take photos at set times. When you put these all together and speed it up, it seems that the plants are growing up out of the ground right before your eyes. This way, they were able to show how bramble stems invade new habitat and use their backwards-facing thorns to grip on to anything they want to climb over. This technique has its risks though – Richard, the cameraman, tried to film a bluebell wood, but came back to his camera to discover a family of mice had nibbled the flowers off all the stems, ruining his shots!

THE VIEW FROM ABOVE

Filming hunting sequences has always been difficult. In the past, camera operators would have to huddle in hides or sneak along in vehicles. By the time *Planet Earth* was being filmed, a show in which David provided commentary, a whole new technology had been developed that used helicopters. Cineflex is a camera set at the bottom of a helicopter that can be operated from within the cockpit, using a joystick to pivot the camera in order to get the shot – importantly, the cameras also come with stabilizers. Before that, helicopters weren't an option because they jiggled too much and long-range cameras require complete stillness. This meant that the team were able to film one of their most famous sequences – African hunting dogs pursuing an antelope.

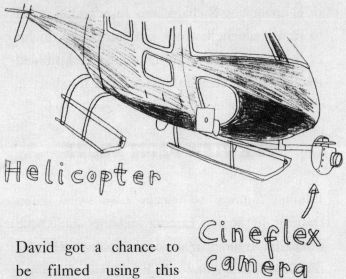

Helicopter

Cineflex camera attached

David got a chance to be filmed using this technology for the 2011 series *Frozen Planet*.

The opening scene would show David at the South Pole close up, then would change to a shot from the aerial camera above, showing him as a tiny speck against the emptiness. But how do you get the Cineflex to the South Pole? They couldn't attach it to the passenger plane David flew in on, or any other helicopter that was being used. They decided to trial attaching it to a small fixed-wing aircraft which they flew to the South Pole.

The next problem was where exactly to film David. Close to the base they were surrounded by flags of countries that had been to Antarctica, which didn't really give the feeling of remoteness they were hoping for. These were originally planted at the South Pole, but due to ice shifting they were now several hundred metres away from it.

The simplest option was for the camera to take to the sky and David to walk along the ice carrying a mobile phone with the camera crew on loudspeaker and wait for them to tell him to stop walking. Not the easiest task for an eighty-year-old, but David was up to it, even though it was thirty-five degrees below freezing outside!

The plane arrived and he spoke a few words about the South Pole; the camera crew asked him for a few more, disappearing and reappearing. Luckily, he soon got the signal that they were all done, and he slowly stomped all the way back to the base.

CLIMATE CHANGE

Just after *The Life of Birds* aired, David produced a programme called *State of the Planet*. The programme was made as a sort of marker for the millennium and looked at the ways humans have impacted our planet. Sort of like a continuation of the last episode of *The Living Planet*.

At the time, this was quite revolutionary. Many people falsely believed then (and do today) that climate change was based on incorrect science or made up. Generally, people were not aware that there was such a thing as climate change which, if you know much about climate change, I can imagine must feel strange to read now.

He made two more programmes in 2006, then again in 2019 and 2020. Now in his nineties, David's focus has shifted firmly towards climate change, on how we can work together to halt its effects and protect all the species that live on our planet.

So, what is climate change? It is long-term change in our global climate that is happening at much faster rates than it would naturally. This affects the temperatures across the world and what types of weather we get, and how often. In places where there are distinct seasons, the start or end of the seasons may shift, or not happen at all.

HOW DO YOU MEASURE THE PAST TEMPERATURE OF THE EARTH?

One way we have been able to measure the average temperature of our planet over time is through ice cores – long cylindrical sections drilled out of the ground.

When ice forms, the snow traps air along with it. By measuring the different concentrations of atmospheric gases in the trapped air, we can work out the average temperatures from the time when the snow fell.

Using this method, scientists have estimated 400,000 years of temperatures and say the ice cores show clear evidence of this temperature increase.

Meanwhile, lots of organizations track the daily temperatures around the world – the Met Office, NASA and the National Oceanic and Atmospheric Administration (NOAA) to name a few.

Combining the data of the past and the present paints a picture of how our climate has changed over time.

Since the 1950s, there has been a very significant increase in average global temperatures. This is called "global warming" and happens because of the natural way the earth traps heat. Gases in our upper atmosphere trap some of the heat that radiates from the planet's surface, bouncing it back down and keeping the planet warm. The problem is that because of human activity, we've started producing lots more of these gases, which stay in our upper atmosphere and trap in more and more heat, meaning our average temperatures go up. We call these gases, which include methane and carbon dioxide, "greenhouse gases".

These gases are released when we burn fossil fuels (oil, gas and coal) to make electricity or run our cars, when burning and decomposing rubbish, and even from our intensive farming systems (I know it sounds weird, but a lot of cows burping and farting has caused a big problem!).

Deforestation is another major contributor, as we cut down forest to raise cattle, and grow soy and oil palms. Trees use carbon dioxide during photosynthesis, the chemical process that helps them create energy, and as we cut down trees we also take away a major store of carbon, meaning more will be in the atmosphere.

This extra carbon also ends up dissolved in the ocean as part of a cycle in which the ocean stores carbon – but so much extra carbon can lead to acidification of the water. Many ocean invertebrates have calcium carbonate shells or outer plates, which can be dissolved by this acidic water. This particularly affects coral reefs, which are vulnerable to something called "bleaching" due to acidification as well as increased temperature.

WHAT IS A CORAL REEF AND WHY DO THEY BLEACH?

While a coral reef might look like a fancy pile of rocks, it's actually a living animal. The structure of a coral reef is made of calcium carbonate, and is an enormous shared exoskeleton laid down to protect the individual coral polyps themselves. It is a living, growing, shared structure that many other animals live in and on.

Coral reefs occupy 0.1 per cent of the ocean but support twenty-five per cent of all marine species, making them extremely important. Sometimes people call them the rainforests of the sea.

coral reef

Inside the corals are tiny microscopic algae called zooxanthellae (zoo-zan-thel-ay) which photosynthesize to create energy and nutrients for the corals. The zooxanthellae are pigmented, so give the corals colour. However, when the temperature rises too much or the water is too acidic, the zooxanthellae leave the coral or die, causing the corals to look pure white. We call this "coral bleaching". Without the zooxanthellae helping corals produce energy, the corals die as well.

Coral bleaching is potentially reversible, but only if coral is protected properly and global warming is halted. When bleached, the corals are unable to support other life, which has a knock-on effect on the local ecosystem.

According to scientists, 2019 was the second hottest year on record (at the time of writing) – and nine of the ten warmest years on record have happened since 2005. Climate change makes these extremes of temperature and also of weather – typhoons, storms, droughts, hurricanes, tornados and monsoons, to name a few – more likely. In the UK in 2017, there was an extended heat wave over the summer, one of the hottest on record, which the Met Office says was made thirty times more likely by the changes in our baseline climate.

These changes in weather and temperature have wide-ranging effects. Increased global temperatures mean that everywhere will start to heat up, which will be most noticeable at our coldest regions around the Arctic and Antarctica. Glaciers are melting from the increased temperature, releasing more water into our oceans and causing sea levels to rise.

This ice also has lots of trapped gases, which could be released and added to the atmosphere. If the ice caps completely melt and our sea levels rise too high, many towns, islands and even whole countries will be flooded. We know that between 1901 and 2010, the average global sea level rose by 20 centimetres. This doesn't sound like much, but it has been enough to affect many low-lying communities – more than ninety per cent of the landmass of Isle de Jean Charles in Louisiana has been submerged.

Higher temperatures also may mean dry countries will be more likely to suffer long droughts and may lose out on their rainy seasons.

Another strange thing that happens in very seasonal places is that the seasons begin to shift. You may have heard people say that it doesn't get as cold as it used to, which is true; our winters are milder. A warmer winter means that the temperature when animals would come out of hibernation or certain plants would sprout might be reached earlier.

While this doesn't sound like too bad a problem, it might mean that the animals and plants fall out of sync with each other.

For example, if moths emerge sooner than they normally do in the year because of an early spring and then die off earlier, woodland birds will be without their main food source for feeding their chicks. Fewer baby birds that year would reach adulthood, meaning a lower population the next year. If that cycle continues, the birds could become endangered.

Most importantly, David wants to shine a light on the people who could change things for the better – politicians, large businesses, heads of state. In some cases, they have downplayed the seriousness of climate change's effects, even though climate scientists agree that human activity has altered our climate and caused these problems.

Sadly, these groups of people who could make a huge positive impact often do nothing because some of them might receive funding and/or benefit in some way from these fossil fuel businesses or have other links to companies and organizations that are contributors to climate change.

"WE'VE BEEN PUTTING THINGS OFF YEAR AFTER YEAR ... THE MOMENT OF CRISIS HAS COME."

In 2008, the UK passed the Climate Change Act, which meant it was a legal duty to ensure the UK lowered its carbon emissions, so that they would be eighty per cent lower than those in 1990 by the year 2050. To do this, there have to be dramatic changes to how businesses, transport systems, and we, as individuals, operate. There have been other agreements between countries like the Kyoto Protocol and the Paris Agreement.

THE PARIS AGREEMENT

The Paris Agreement is a protocol signed by countries in which they agreed to combat climate change, and to speed up the investments and actions required so that we use less fossil fuels.

Crucially, it also says that wealthy countries have to take the most action so that other countries have time to build and develop the infrastructure these wealthy countries already have. This is called "climate equity".

The main aim is to keep the global

temperature rise over the next 100 years to less than 2°C, with the intention to limit the rise to 1.5°C.

In 2017, climate scientists warned that we only have three years to reverse growth in greenhouse gas emissions to meet the goals of the Paris Agreement.

David, scientists and climate activists, like Greta Thunberg and Vanessa Nakate, say that we are running out of time to make big enough changes that will meet these targets and slow the effects of global warming. Essentially, the longer we wait, the more difficult a problem it will be to solve. Especially if we reach a what scientists call "tipping points" in which the change has grown so much that it causes a spiral of catastrophic further changes. These are much more difficult to predict and may be irreversible.

GRETA THUNBERG

- Swedish schoolgirl Greta Thunberg (born 3 January 2003) has gradually become a recognizable and respected voice in the climate change movement.

- When Greta was eight years old, she learned about climate change and vowed to do something to stop it.

- Inspired by the American students who had protested gun violence after a shooting happened at their school, Greta decided a school strike for the climate could be just as effective. On Friday, 20 August 2018, armed with a placard that said "SKOLSTREJK FÖR KLIMATET", Greta sat alone in front of the Riksdag, the seat of Swedish Parliament.

- After she spoke about the strike on social media, other students in Sweden began to join her. Eventually the School Strike for Climate (also known as Fridays for Future) became an international movement.

- Greta is now a well-respected speaker on climate change issues, having spoken at meetings including at the United Nations Climate Change Conference.

- Many of her speeches have gone viral on social media and in 2018, a collection of them was published under the title *No One is Too Small to Make a Difference*.

- Greta is autistic, and says that "To be different is not a weakness. It's a strength in many ways, because you stand out from the crowd."

VANESSA NAKATE

- Vanessa Nakate (born 15 November 1996) is a Ugandan activist and advocate of climate justice.

- She founded Youth for Future Africa and the Africa-based Rise Up Movement.

- Taking inspiration from Greta Thunberg,

Nakate began her own solitary strike against inaction on the climate crisis outside of the Parliament of Uganda in January 2019.

• She fights to draw attention to climate change, specifically damage to the Congolian rainforest (the world's second largest rainforest, spanning six countries) caused by heat and drought, as well as the effects that climate change has on agriculture, which Uganda heavily depends on. "So, if our farms are destroyed by floods, if the farms are destroyed by droughts and crop production is less, that means the price of food is going to go high. So it will only be the most privileged who will be able to buy food."

• She also uses her voice to elevate those of other Black activists and to bring the issues caused in Africa by climate change – which are often forgotten or ignored by the West – to the forefront.

There are lots of things that can be done to reduce or prevent the effects of climate change, including using alternative green energy systems, planting more trees, and creating ways to capture the extra carbon in the atmosphere. We would need to change the way businesses and agriculture are run, and create new technologies to manage extreme weather events, and create defences against the higher sea level. There is a lot that can be done, but we must act now.

Now you've read this book and learned about all the wonderful things living on our planet hopefully you, like David, will want to stop climate change. While the big changes have to come from our politicians and businesses, there are also some things that you can do:

1. Turn the lights off when you don't need them and be careful of how much hot water you use. Don't waste your resources. Got a stale glass of water sitting on the dinner table? Water the plants with it.

2. Use public transport instead of cars where and when you can or share a ride with someone else.

3. The five Rs: Refuse, Reduce, Reuse, Repurpose and Recycle.

4. Think about the food you eat. There are things you could do – like eat more seasonal veg and be aware of the packaging your food comes in. Any change, no matter how small, is a good change!

5. Find ways to repurpose things you've already got, rather than throwing them away. For example, you can learn to mend tears and holes in your clothes to make them last longer.

6. Recycle everything you can. Many places have different recycling rules, so make sure you know what will be collected and when.

Some places will even take fabric scraps, used batteries and electronics. Ask an adult for help on where to start!

7. Make your voice heard. Write to politicians and ask them to keep to their promises and legal requirements of the Climate Change Act to tackle climate change. Your voice matters and you deserve to be listened to.

Over the last sixty years, Sir David Attenborough has shown us the full range of life on the planet we call home, from the most beautiful creatures to the strangest, and those most desperately in need of our protection.

Now it's our turn to listen, to learn and to act and work together to save our planet.

TIMELINE OF DAVID ATTENBOROUGH'S LIFE

1926 Born on 8 May in Isleworth

1947 Graduates from Cambridge University with a degree in Natural Sciences

1950 Marries Jane Oriel

1952 Joins the BBC full-time

1954 *Zoo Quest to West Africa*

1955 *Zoo Quest to Guiana*

1956 *Zoo Quest for a Dragon*

1957 *Zoo Quest for the Paradise Birds*

1965 Becomes controller of BBC Two

1972 Awarded the Royal Geographical Society's Cherry Kearton Medal and Award for his work in natural history

1977–2005 Narrates *Wildlife on One*, a series where each episode is made by a new filmmaker

1979 *Life on Earth* airs

1980 Awarded a BAFTA Fellowship for lifetime achievement in filmmaking

1981 Wins the Kalinga Prize for the Popularisation of Science from UNESCO

1983 Elected a Fellow of the Royal Society

1984 *The Living Planet* airs

1985 Knighted by Queen Elizabeth II. (He already held a CBE, and would go on to be awarded a CVO, a CH and an OM. His full name is now very, very long.)

1990 *The Trials of Life* airs

1991–96 President of the Royal Society of Nature Conservation

1993 An extinct class of pliosaurid (a type of marine reptile) from the Early Jurassic period of Dorset, England, is named *Attenborosaurus*, after Sir David Attenborough

1995 *The Private Life of Plants* airs

1998 *The Life of Birds* airs

1996 Wins Kew International Medal

2000 *State of the Planet* airs

2000 Wins International Cosmos Prize and RSPB Medal

2001 *Blue Planet* airs

2002 *The Life of Mammals* airs

2006 *Planet Earth* airs

2006 *The Truth about Climate Change* airs

2008 *Life in Cold Blood* airs and the Royal Photographic Society awards David its Progress Medal and an Honorary Fellowship in recognition of his work

2009 Co-writes *Life*

2011 *Frozen Planet* airs

2012 Awarded the IUCN Phillips Memorial Medal for outstanding service in international conservation

2016 British polar research vessel is named after him, the RRS *Sir David Attenborough* (though public votes wanted RRS *Boaty McBoatface*)

2017 *Blue Planet II* airs

2018 and 2019 Wins a Primetime Emmy for Outstanding Narrator for *Blue Planet II* and *Our Planet*

2019 *Our Planet; Seven Worlds, One Planet* and *Climate Change – The Facts* air

ABOUT THE AUTHOR

Lizzie Huxley-Jones is an autistic writer and editor based in London. Growing up watching as many David Attenborough programmes as possible, she went on to study zoology at university, which led her to work as a research diver in the Philippines, at an ecological centre in Honduras and for a charity supporting small-scale fishers around the world from her desk in London. Now a full-time writer, she is the editor of *Stim*, an anthology of autistic authors and artists, and works to champion disabled voices in literature, in between walking her dog, Nerys. Her favourite animal is the red fox.

GLOSSARY

Acidification: the process by which something becomes more acidic.

Asexual reproduction: a type of reproduction where one parent passes on all their genetic material to their offspring. For a cell this might mean splitting in half. In animals, rather than two parents mixing up half their genetic material together, the offspring inherits all the genes of their single parent.

Birder: someone who likes to go birdwatching as a hobby.

Captive breeding programme: a system run by some zoos where they breed lots of one animal with the intention of releasing some of them back into the wild, or to ensure the continuation of the species until that is possible.

Clergyman: a man who works in the Christian church, usually a priest or a minister.

Climate: the name for the long-term (usually about thirty years) average weather of a place, including temperature, rainfall, humidity, air pressure and wind.

Climate change: change in the long-term average weather (or climate) of a single place (regional) or the whole world (global). When we talk about climate change happening now, we are referring to the process by which the climate is changing at faster rates than it would naturally change.

Commonwealth: this was a group of countries, most of which had been colonized and ruled by the British and are now independent.

Echidnas: a small spiny mammal that looks a little like a hedgehog with a longer snout. They are one of the few mammals that lay eggs. There are four species of echidna and all are found in Australia, New Guinea and Tasmania.

Echolocation: using sound to work out how far away objects are by listening to the echoes as sound bounces off that object. Bats, dolphins and even some kinds of shrew use echolocation to navigate, hunt and find other members of their species. Some blind people have also learned to use echolocation by clicking their tongues.

Ecosystem: the name for the physical features of a place plus the animals and plants living within that place and interacting with it.

Ectothermic: animals who cannot produce body heat themselves, and so have to take it in from external sources like sunlight or a heated surface. We sometimes call these animals "cold-blooded".

Endothermic: animals that can produce their own body heat, which is done by converting the food they eat into heat energy. Humans are endothermic – congratulations. We sometimes call them "warm-blooded".

Environment: the natural world as a whole, or a particular area affected by human activity. Sometimes the word environment is used in place of "ecosystem".

Evolution: the idea that all living things on earth are updated versions of other living things from the past, with changes happening slowly over generations. This slow process of change in genes over time in all living creatures leads to new species.

Extinction: when a species completely dies out and no more remain alive. "Extinct in the wild" means that species only exists in zoos, while "functionally extinct" means there aren't enough of a species left to keep the population as a whole alive, and that they will very likely become extinct.

Fossil record: our entire knowledge of fossils found over the world, including what time period in history they were around for and when they became extinct, and how they relate to other species.

Fossils: evidence of animals or plants from the past that have been preserved over time and can be viewed today. This evidence can be their remains (shells, bones, exoskeletons) or imprints, like footsteps or the shape of animals' bodies which have since rotted.

Gender dysphoria: when someone has a gender identity that doesn't necessarily align with their sex, and so may experience serious distress about their outside appearance not matching up to how they feel on the inside.

Genes: sections of DNA inside your cells which carry specific instructions about how to build particular parts of you.

Genetics: a term for all your genes and how they relate to your body, for example, your genetic make-up. The science of studying genes is also called genetics.

Geology: the scientific study of the earth – how it changes and is formed over time, and the rocks and minerals that make up the planet.

Geophone: a device that records ground movement and converts it from velocity, or speed in a particular direction, to voltage so that scientists can study it.

Habitat: the specific environment that an animal or plant lives in. Your home, and the town you live in, is your habitat.

Incubate: how animals who lay eggs help their offspring develop. By keeping the eggs warm, the baby animals (or embryos) inside can grow. Some animals use their body heat, some bury the eggs and some build big nests.

Invertebrate: animals that do not have a spine, and may instead have a protective exoskeleton or shell, such as spiders, octopuses, snails and worms are all invertebrates.

Landforms: mountains, hills, plateaus and plains.

Larva: a young form of an animal that will later undergo metamorphosis (a huge change in their body). For example, caterpillars are the larval form of a butterfly, and tadpoles are the larval form of a frog.

Lekking: a type of mating display where males perform (often against each other) to compete for females to mate with.

Mammals: all species of vertebrate animals that are warm-blooded and produce milk for their offspring. They often have hair or fur, and usually give birth to live young. There are some mammals that lay eggs, like echidnas and platypuses.

Natural selection: the idea that animals that are well-adapted to their environment are more likely to reproduce, thus passing on their good genes to their offspring who will also be well-adapted to the environment. This means that species are not fixed and can change over time, in response to the environment they live in.

Nocturnal: animals that are awake and active at night.

Offspring: an animal's babies.

Omnivore: an animal that eats plants and other animals.

Petrification: the process of something turning to stone.

Phobia: an extreme and intense – possibly irrational – fear of something.

Poachers: people who illegally hunt in nature reserves or target protected species.

Pollution: the introduction of poisonous or harmful materials into the environment. Pollution can be chemicals, but also noise, light and sound. These can disrupt how ecosystems work and harm the animals and plants within them.

Radiometric dating: a way of dating rocks and fossils by detecting atoms we know a lot about that are trapped inside and very slowly break down. By looking at how broken down the atoms are, we can estimate how old the rocks are.

Renewable resources: an energy source that can be used repeatedly and the amount that is used is very easily replenished (or refilled), though this process sometimes has to be controlled to make sure we don't use too much. Examples of this are solar energy from the sun, hydropower from water and burning wood.

Savannah: an ecosystem made up of open grassland and very widely spaced trees.

Species: a group of animals or plants with shared characteristics and genes that can reproduce together to create offspring who can also reproduce, or are fertile.

Studbook: all the information used by captive breeding programmes about who an animal's family members are, going back several generations.

Sub-species: two groups of a single species are split into sub-species when they are separated geographically, and so live in two different places, with separate diets and habitats. The extra name distinguishes which group they are.

Tectonic plates: pieces of the earth's crust and mantle, or upper layers.

Teleprompters: screens in front of a television presenter that show the script as they need to say it.

Trophic cascade: a large sudden change in an ecosystem due to one species dying out or invading, which impacts the other species within the ecosystem. This can cause dramatic changes to food webs or even cause the ecosystem to collapse.

Vertebrate: an animal that has a backbone or spinal column, such as mammals, birds, reptiles, amphibians and fish.

BIBLIOGRAPHY AND FURTHER READING

Attenborough, David (2010)
Life on Air
BBC Books

Attenborough, David (2017)
Adventures of a Young Naturalist: The Zoo Quest Expeditions
Two Roads, Hachette UK

Attenborough, David (2018)
Journeys to the Other Side of the World
Two Roads, Hachette UK

Dyu, Lily (2019)
Earth Heroes
Nosy Crow

Thunberg, Greta (2018)
No One is Too Small to Make a Difference
Penguin Books UK

INDEX

LOOK OUT FOR

ROSALIND FRANKLIN

Science and everyday life cannot and should NOT be separated.

A LIFE STORY

DNA Pioneer

ALAN TURING

I propose to consider the question, 'Can machines think?'

A LIFE STORY

Computer Scientist